POETIC INQUIRY FOR SYNCHRONY & LOVE

A NEW ORDER OF GRAVITY

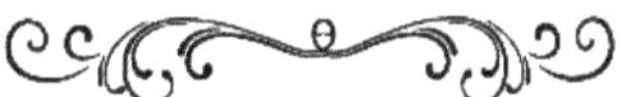

MYTHOPOETIC IMAGINATION

Series Editor: Alexandra Fidyk

POETIC INQUIRY FOR SYNCHRONY & LOVE

A NEW ORDER OF GRAVITY

ALEXANDRA FIDYK
DARLENE ST. GEORGES

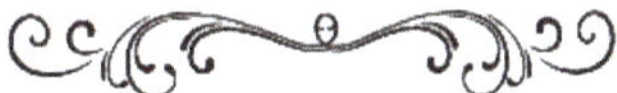

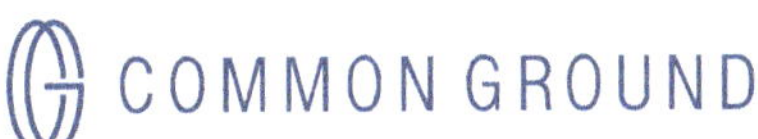

First published in 2025 as part of **Arts in Society Book Imprint**
Common Ground Research Networks
University of Illinois Research Park 2001 South First St, Suite 20 L Champaign, IL 61820 USA

Library of Congress Cataloging-in-Publication Data

Names: Fidyk, Alexandra, author. | St. Georges, Darlene, author.
Title: Poetic inquiry for synchrony & love : a new order of gravity / Alexandra Fidyk & Darlene St. Georges [editors].
Description: Champaign, IL : Common Ground Research Networks, [2024] | Series: Mythopoetic imagination | Includes bibliographical references.
Identifiers: LCCN 2024059739 (print) | LCCN 2024059740 (ebook) | ISBN 9781966214304 (hbk) | ISBN 9781966214311 (pbk) | ISBN 9781966214328 (pdf)
Subjects: LCSH: Canadian poetry. | Reflection (Philosophy)--Poetry. | Self--Poetry. | Poetics. | Reflection (Philosophy) in literature. | Self in literature.
Classification: LCC PR9195.25 P64 2025 (print) | LCC PR9195.25 (ebook) | DDC 808.1--dc23/eng/20250121
LC record available at https://lccn.loc.gov/2024059739
LC ebook record available at https://lccn.loc.gov/2024059740

Cover Image & Design: Darlene St. Georges

POETIC CONTENT

DEDICATION

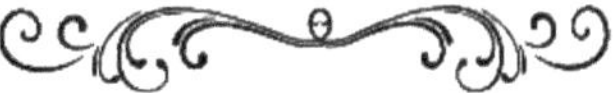

To all things animate…

EDITORS' NOTES

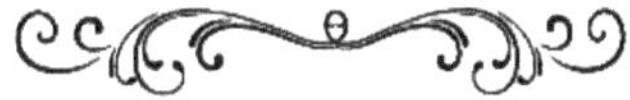

April, 2025
Alexandra Fidyk
Edmonton, Alberta

Tethered to the Round
Her movements turn the world
with rhythmic certainty, they
foretell love and grief

In our edited collection, Poetic Inquiry is positioned *as a way of becoming with an animate, agential cosmos*. This positioning, informed by theoretical, philosophical, experiential, and ethical understanding, does not reflect an ontological turn in the field; rather, it critically claims a place that has always already been. Simultaneously, it is other than the dominant perspectives historically held within Poetic Inquiry. To date, Poetic Inquiry publications and research in education, the humanities, and social sciences have not explicitly recognized this vital orientation regarding the nature of existence. Certainly, many of the poet-authors gathered in the following pages have long belonged to this positionality but their writings, images, and ideas may not have been ontologically and axiologically differentiated by Poetic Inquiry publications, communities, and other research hubs. This animate world and its cosmic neighbours enfold through a creative process of relational becoming—an art of dynamic form—germinally aesthetic.

As described in our sister publication, Poetic Inquiry for Synchrony & Love: A New Order of Gravity, Special Issue, *Art|Research International: A Transdisciplinary Journal* (2022), when faced with the challenge of publishing poetic, artistic, storying research in discipline-based journals—such as, educational research, curriculum studies, and arts education—many of us have met the rub of ontological tension. That is, when writing with intuition, embodiment, embeddedness, and feeling, and when working from the imaginal, ancestral, and relational fields, we often have encountered misunderstandings, even misplaced criticisms due to paradigmatic comparisons. These include a range of misses from editors and publishers not knowing where to position our work within a particular context; how we position ourselves as scholars; in what ways our research meets expectations or not; and, how to understand what research is and how it can be demonstrated. Additionally, the imposition of scholarly structures and standards that reflect hegemonic standpoints, such as reviewer templates with one-size-fits-all criteria, amplify obstacles. These templates continue to reflect values inherent to post-positivist paradigms—reflecting a knower and not-knower antagonism or requiring a methodology for example—and seek to steer research into the very binaries and boxes that some poets, authors, artists, and researchers have or are striving to abandon.

This growing and unresolved problematic across the last two decades is becoming increasingly untenable, even non-negotiable, for authors living in animate ontologies (for instance, Indigenous Knowledge Systems, Wisdom Traditions, analytical psychology, and process-relational philosophy) enacted through research belonging to an evolving continuum of burgeoning paradigms. Such non-negotiation is bidirectional where authors, whose research pushes the boundaries of modernity (causal, predictable, and measurable) and post-modernity (subjective, fragmentary, and without metanarratives), who cannot for their own integrity and for that of their work distort their research to fit into conflicting ontologies and cosmologies. On the other hand, when submissions challenge editors' and publishers' currency (funding, reputation, analytics), move too far from their established disciplines, or exist upon unfamiliar ground, they are rejected. In response to these challenges, our love of poetics and Poetic Inquiry, as well as our reverence for animate onto-ethical-epistemologies, we called to our growing international Poetic Inquiry community to write from this beckoning centre. This centre has 'A New Order of Gravity,' a weight, that binds us to the here and now while beholding the fluid past and the already manifesting tomorrow. This ethic asks us to bear witness to that "strange intimacy between grief and aliveness" (Lerner in Weller, 2025, p. xii)—an attending that promises to deepen the arc of our lives even amidst a world raging with war, injustice, poverty, and religious strife.

Wind whistles under Her wing
great feathered expanse
She enfolds it all
while granite smoke rises

To credit this centre as animate (peripheral to dominant polities) and with the expansive and inclusive dimensions of poetics and poetry, we called for Poetic Inquiry research that respects the sovereignty of creative generativity. That is, research that honours a dynamic world pulsating in-to and out-of existence; that abides with the ancestral, reciprocal, and imaginal realms; that beholds paradox, liminality, and synchronicity; that privileges intuitive, embodied, somatic, and affective ways of knowing; and that mirrors the fibrous weave of cosmic interdependence and interrelatedness. Our edited collection called for poetic words, poetic images, poetic forms, and poetic arrangements that acknowledge the transdirectionality of the birth, death, and rebirth—of poplar, wind, and bone. We called for poetics that explore what is precious, bejeweled; what is refracted, light; what is of and for humility, sacred—with the intention to offer a curative for catastrophic times. We called for 'Synchrony and Love.'

As enacted synchrony between our two publications, Darlene and I engaged in co-creative processes with the authors' submitted works published in our special issue in *Art|Research International.* With author permission, we collected poetic clusters from each published text and wove them as poems through this imprint. These pages include poetic images of feathers—extending particularities of prairie places through the presence of the crows in our cover image—and offering imagistic embodiment as Poetic Inquiry. Doing so not only demonstrates inclusivity, relationality, and decolonizing practice, but also it circumvents the publishing practice of separate and singular scholarship. Here, we plaited poems from the online open access journal with the first Poetic Inquiry edited collection that does not require authors to expound upon their poetic and lyric texts as has been the publishing requirement to date. That is, poems, the poetic, and lyric enact research, and within this view of reality do not require explication. Our curation also bespeaks a mirroring practice where included works echo the lived body particularities of synchrony, love, and gravity as poets, authors, and scholars transverse the world of matter, spirit, and meaning. The collection reiterates select works where circling embodies a ceremony of renewal; a practice known well through the acts of remembrance and mourning. This way of turning, of revisiting, asks that we consider the kind of attention we offer as "attention changes *what kind of* a thing comes into being for us: in that way, it changes the world" (McGilchrist, 2009, p. 28, emphasis in original). That is, a world that has not come into being as a collection of static "things"; rather, a world composed of things becoming as events and processes, of many to the one. A world that reflects a patterning in the universe, in us, and in the ancient coupling of "aesthetic" and "ethic." In its pre-Christian form, aesthetic "referred to the right placing of the multiple things in the world" (Hillman, 1992, p. 43), even if that arrangement was ugly, frightful (Fidyk, 2018, p. 211). Here, bearing witness to extremes can bring us to beauty—to "the luster of each particular event" (Hillman, 1992, p. 43). As James Hillman (1992) put it, beauty is "the very sensibility of the cosmos; its . . . textures, tones, tastes" (p. 43).

Translucent moon
hanging low
reflects light, patient

blue dawn returns—

Historically, Poetic Inquiry was positioned under the umbrella of Arts-Based Research (ABR) and Arts-Based Educational Research (ABER) through Monica Prendergast's post-doctoral research. It built upon "the methodological interests and contributions of her graduate work in the field of arts-based research approaches, specifically in the sub-field of poetic forms of inquiry" (Prendergast, 2007, personal communication May 30). Prendergast's "meta-analytical cross-disciplinary study on the methodological value of using poetry, as both art and research, in qualitative inquiry," (Prendergast, 2007, personal communication) spotlighted the term 'poetic inquiry' from among numerous terms for the same as outlined in her annotated bibliography (Prendergast, 2009, p. xx-xxi). She systematized her findings "found in many areas of the social sciences: psychology, sociology, anthropology, nursing, social work, geography, women's/feminist studies and education" (p. xxi) via the categories of *vox theoria*, *vox autobiographia* or *autoethnographia*, and *vox participare*, with corresponding percentages denoting their appearance as figured in "statistics on poetic inquiry" (p. xix). Her early work offered "a guide" to "the how-to of writing poetic inquiry" (Prendergast, 2009, p. xxiii) through a synthesis of work by researchers, including Carl Leggo, Laurel Richardson, Ivan Brady, whom had been doing poetic practice across their own scholarship. The uncovering of poetry in research defined as "*poems* published in peer-reviewed qualitative research journals" (Prendergast, 2007) and their coordinated schematic framing as method was, and continues to be, an invaluable offering to the social sciences, especially within modernist and post-modernist research paradigms. Her post-doctoral research revealed, what I assume to be, previously unimagined possibilities for many artists, poets, and researchers. As an invited doctoral student who presented at the first International Symposium on Poetic Inquiry (2007), it was an electric moment that has continued to foster development and diversification within the research approach through evolving aims, practices, and values.

My presentation, *Addressing Silence & the Sea: Poetic Musings with Pablo Neruda* (2007, 2009), given at the inaugural event, embodied mythopoetic remembering, animate ontology, and insights gleaned from Whiteheadian process-relational philosophy. At this first formal gathering of doing poetic research in the social sciences, I enacted Poetic Inquiry as a way of living in relation to the dead, blood memory, the unconscious, and my kinship with place: Colombia (students, histories, land, war). As I repositioned in our *Art|Research International* editorial, Poetic Inquiry enacted from animate ontologies is knowing-being-becoming-valuing that arises from "poetic consciousness" (Fidyk, 2006, p. iii) where epistemologies and ethics *cannot* be separated from this view of reality. As such, poetic inquiring has long appeared in research that may or may not include poems. Naming and quantifying poems do not legitimize its usage except in paradigms that adhere to said standards. That is, *poetics* connotes more than verse—as image and or structure; a "poem" *does not* determine if the work (research and scholarship) is poetic or Poetic Inquiry. Additionally, if poetics manifests from the unconscious and or kinds of consciousness other than the egoic, it cannot be contained nor directed by methodologies and methods, troubling the claims made by the historic ABR and ABER Poetic Inquiry positioning. As a form of consciousness, a way of being and becoming, poetics, poems, and poetic inquiring exist outside of arts-based research. Stated otherwise, Poetic Inquiry can but does not have to be located under the umbrella of ABR and ABER—it can stand as the research approach guiding the research design. This ontological delineation is a fundamental positioning and unnamed among the work of poets, artists, and researchers in the field.

azure, arctic, denim, cerulean, lapis, cobalt, and slate
sensorial tastes of dawn
of water and sky, call us
through symbolic ritual
        to repeat Her gestures

Poetic unfolding through animate relationality has been ignored across our research communities' publications and gatherings which consistently highlight epistemologies, methodologies (also undertheorized), and methods while remarkably ignoring ontologies and cosmologies. Reviewers of Poetic Inquiry publications have requested submissions to demarcate poems from prose text—as if a poem, literary or otherwise, verified the works' poetic validity. When a doctoral student, I was perplexed when this initially happened (Fidyk, 2009) as I could not comprehend how poetic rumination, exploration, contemplation, and imagination was conceptualized. In my interpretation, my prose texts having an imaginative and emotionally attuned style of expression were poetry, poetic expressions—lyric, rhythmic, symbolic, aesthetic. In this way, differentiation of what Poetic Inquiry is and can be across research positionalities may embolden poets, authors, and scholars to deepen their emplacement and their relations regardless of paradigm or worldview. Thus, this collection champions Poetic Inquiry that reflects a post-post-modern universe, engaging poetry not as arts-based, qualitative research, or methodological value, but as poetic consciousness, as "relational consciousness" (Fidyk, 2006, p. iii). Such reconstitution through remembrance, for example, reflects human consciousness emerging *with* the natural world, where it, for many human collectives, slowly transitioned from forms of fusion or oneness with particular geographies to more distinct versions of being where people recognize no connection with the ecosystems in which they live. Poetic Inquiring or co-inquiring here places us in a non-competitive, non-hierarchical relationship with the earth (cosmos) and stresses the values of mutuality, respect, community, relational accountability, shared governance, humility, and love—which brings no threat to individuality and subjectivity—despite its transsubjective dimension. My continued effort to differentiate ontologies rendered by Poetic Inquiry has and continues to respect *both and* modern, post-modern, and post-post-modern research positions in "a disciplined act of attending to things" (Fidyk, 2018, p. 34). Doing so benefits the field in an "ontologically robust" (Zwicky, 2008, p. 86) effort to keep us aligned with communities of events and processes, with radical relatedness.

Mythic remembering recalls a self
that feels itself to be rememberingly—
a connective self-creating itself
out of the elements of the world

—of the many to the one

Poetic consciousness, as called forth here, enfolds myth, symbol, oratory, allegory, story, metaphor, prophecy, analogy, metonym, theatre, music, and ritual while it unfolds in a particular place-time-body. In the earliest notes of human languages, poetics was expressed through oratorial traditions: mimicry, song, chant, prayer, creation story, myth—and myriad forms of visual and then written expression: cuneiform script on wet clay using reed markings, papyrus, and oracle bone. Within animate ontologies (Fidyk 2006, 2007, 2009, 2013, 2017, 2018), we retrieve the ancient practice of leading forth from poetic consciousness and poetics—that is, being and becoming through song, image, and metaphor in relation to one's immediacy. These forms of human being bring us feelingly into creative becoming with all elements through body-and-place to consciousness.

in-gathering intimate-ghosts
revelatory kinships, family resemblances
lost places, necessary silences, and
bird song on the grace of dew

From this taproot, Poetic Inquiry reveals itself as an enlivened and enlivening approach to research where it remains true unto itself. Poetic inquiring as such cannot be severed from its kin and ground; Poetic inquiring keeps poet, place, phenomenon, and the implicate order that organizes and holds them in webbed interdependence. Poetic inquiring extends from the arrival of a question or through the midst of a problem into wondering, noticing, imaging, attending, and so on, if and until it breaks forth in one or more intentional and or spontaneous forms of expression. To inquire is ontological. To poeticize is ontological. Neither can be severed from ways of knowing and valuing (Fidyk, 2013, 2017). In this way of animate ontologies, Poetic Inquiry cannot be a methodology because "[m]ethodology works through decontextualization where methods separate or distance subject and object, the researcher and the researched" (Usher, 1996, p. 40). Likewise, Poetic Inquiry cannot be the formalized and standardized use of methods to systematically address and investigate pre-defined issues or problems. As an organic, iterative gestalt, Poetic Inquiry, then, cannot be compartmentalized as a means to analyze data or represent data, as this stands in isolation from its organic event of co-rising. Thus, Poetic Inquiry cannot be (used as) a tool to play with data. When it is attempted, Poetic Inquiry collapses—away from its relations and into a dualistic paradigm most often qualitative and humanistic. This abstraction and Poetic Inquiry's common usage works to maintain the assumption of an independently existing and knowable reality. When methods claim and tell, perhaps through poetic words and forms, as a data chapter or section within a methodology, they lead to generalizations and conclusions that sever the fecund particularities of studies. While Poetic Inquiry can enact rigor, it does not seek to eliminate reflexivity. Reflexivity, as a "bending back on itself" (Usher, 1996, p. 48), enables us to interrogate our own practices of research in ways that can become part of dominant and oppressive discourses, especially in educational research. Poetic Inquiry calls forth the embodied and embedded of the personal and what lies beyond it while interconnected with the social, cultural, political, ecological, ethical, and transpersonal.

parallel matrices of feather and shore
encompass the subtle stages between
the polar axes of birth and decay
Earth's rhythm, Life's rhythm, Hers—

Poetic Inquiry as animate does not claim to know what to do in the tangle of an issue, but it does trust that something will happen and the next movement will unfold. Poetic Inquiry as animate asks us to tarry, to tend. So, when we were faced with the challenges related to the global COVID-19 pandemic, Darlene and I penned a call to serve as a communal curative. Understanding that the world as we knew it had been destabilized, we sought to attune to fresh patterns arising. The poet-authors gathered here challenge the taken-for-granted understandings about Poetic Inquiry and press us to continue to imagine the field anew. They attend patterns of the known, unknown, and yet to be known, while serving collective rhythms and enacting an ethic of care. Poetic Inquiry, a fluxing, enfolding, generative way to research continues to cross ontological, epistemological, ethical, and axiological lines, while weaving germane configurations. These nameable elements birthed the image of Poetic Inquiry for synchrony and love.

the rhythm of time
and of procession confirm
the most primitive intuition—
that death is return

References

Fidyk, A. (2018). "A setting of things side by side." In P. Sameshima, A. Fidyk, K. James, & C. Leggo (Eds.), *Poetic Inquiry: Enchantment of place* (pp. 32-37). Vernon Press.

Fidyk, A. (2018). An aesthetic of the underworld. In P. Sameshima, A. Fidyk, K. James, & C. Leggo (Eds.), *Poetic Inquiry: Enchantment of place* (pp. 211-219). Vernon Press.

Fidyk, A. (2017). *Locating research in an animated world: Re-conceptualizing design.* Lusophone Scientific Repository. http://hdl.handle.net/10437/7624

Fidyk, A. (2013). Conducting research in an animated world: A case *for* suffering. *International Journal of Multiple Research Approaches, 7*(3), 378-391.

Fidyk, A. (2009). Addressing Silence & the Sea: Poetic musings with Pablo Neruda. *Educational Insights, 13*(3), 1-12. Available: https://citeseerx.ist.psu.edu/document?repid=rep1&type=pdf&doi=3038dc55e4a6bd36c7684780d2a04e6701a8b748

Fidyk, A. (2007). *Addressing Silence & the Sea: Poetic musings with Pablo Neruda.* Invited presentation at the International Symposium on Poetic Inquiry at the Centre for Cross-Faculty Inquiry, Faculty of Education, University of British Columbia, Vancouver, BC.

Fidyk, A. (2006). *Silence and eros: Beckoning the background forward.* [Unpublished doctoral dissertation]. University of Calgary. https://prism.ucalgary.ca/handle/1880/101595

Fidyk, A., & St. Georges, D. (Eds.). (2022). Editorial. Poetic Inquiry for Synchrony & Love: A New Order of Gravity, Special Issue. *Art|Research International: A Transdisciplinary Journal, 7*(2), ix-xv.

Hillman, J. (1992). *The thought of the heart and the soul of the world.* Spring Publications.

Lerner, M. (2025). Foreword. In F. Weller, *The wild edge of sorrow. Rituals of renewal and the sacred work of grief.* North Atlantic Books.

McGilchrist, I. (2009). *The master and his emissary: The divided brain and the making of the western world.* Yale University Press.

Prendergast, M. (2009). Introduction: The phenomena of poetry in research. In M. Prendergast, C. Leggo, & P. Sameshima (Eds.), *Poetic Inquiry: Vibrant voices in the social sciences* (pp. xix-xlii). Sense Publishers.

Prendergast, M. (2007). *Poetic inquiry: An annotated bibliography.* Centre for Cross-Faculty Inquiry, Faculty of Education, University of British Columbia.

Usher, R. (1996). Textuality and reflexivity in educational research. In D. Scott & R. Usher (Eds.). *Understanding educational research* (pp. 33-51). Routledge.

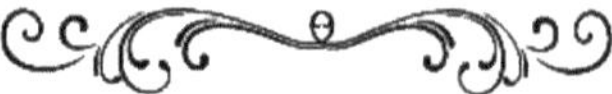

April 2025
Darlene St. Georges
Lethbridge, Alberta

Poetic Inquiry situated in an animated and "creation-centered paradigm" (St. Georges 2024)—an aesthetic-relational paradigm that advocates for exploration and expression of our subjectivities—our becoming—through our inward and outward journeys. The turn inward to understand realities of existence is a different incorporeal knowledge paradigm (Ermine, 1996). It activates a type of metaphorical dialectic through the visual, textual, imaginal, haptic, and ethereal. The infinity of difference found in our own humanity, without paper and pencil, without clock, without competitive comparison is what Maori have called *aromatawai* (self-reflection) that instructs and transforms (Meyers, 2013), which is inherently relational. Subjective experience and knowing in learning and development is an integral symbiotic process of both ones' personal evolution and our collective growth. Each person's process of becoming through subjective introspective experience is relationally connected—what I know, learn and share honours my connections with others and benefits the whole community: family, friends, schools, neighbourhood, ecosystems and so on (St. Georges, 2019).

She wades knee deep
embodying the murmuration of spirits
who follow Her

imperceptibly

(St. Georges, 2024)

The potential of this type of poetic inquiry and encounters invite explorations of knowledge(s) rooted in memory and experience, internal knowing, (in)sight and vision, and gives rise to forms of thinking that are metaphorical, divergent, and ambiguous which can hold multiple meaning and usher in forms of psyche life into perceptual awareness. Through juxtaposition, metaphor, euphemism and suggestion, this poetic inquiring opens up spaces to discover and unveil or keep hidden and obscure—creating spaces to wrestle with the complexities of being (St. Georges, 2019).

Poetic inquiry situated in an animated and creation-centered paradigm is a proposition to shift away from norms and conventions precisely by engaging subjectively in aesthetic, spiritual, intellectual and embodied ways (St. Georges, 2024).

She cradles her bundle
of sacred text, thick in premise
that shield Her yellow orchard body

the old ones
that hum without hesitancy
in crimson chambers—

(St. Georges, 2024)

References

Ermine, W. (1996). Aboriginal epistemology. In M. Battiste, & M. Barmand (Eds.), *First Nations education in Canada: The circle unfolds* (pp. 101-112). UBC Press.

Meyer, M. A. (2013). Holographic epistemology Native common sense. *China Media Research*, *9*(2), 94-101.

St. Georges, D. (2024). She-Hero: A memoir of the Divine Feminine within a creation-centred paradigm. In *Artizein: Arts and Teaching Journal, 9*(1), 88-113.

St. Georges, D. (2024). Embodied landscapes: A creation-centred métissage of self-in-relation. In J. Markides, & D. St. Georges (Eds.), *Arts creation: A curriculum of relationality, resurgence and renewal* (pp. 347-375). DOI Press.

St. Georges, D. (2019). Relational poetic encounters: Opening spaces at the Tate Liverpool. *International Journal of Art and Design Education*, *38*(3), 710-722. DOI:10.1111/jade.12249.

Alexandra Fidyk

Storyteller

There—
against the frozen windscape,
against the freeze-frame of lake, its vast expanse
white on white, adorned, encased
by ice crystals and reflected light,
        his shining blue-black feathers
        radiant with life.

He hopped on the snow-packed earth, stealing
bits of this and that, scraps unseen
by any other eye,

divining the story of this land.

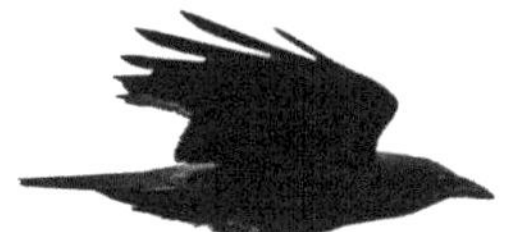

Patricia Reis

Feeding the Spirits

When someone lifts us
He lifts in his hand millions of memories
Which do not dissolve in blood
Like evening

—*Chorus of the Stones,* Nelly Sachs

It is late August, and I am co-leading a Dreamquest canoe trip on Lake Aziscohos in western Maine with my friend, Anne, a Maine guide. We are eighteen women in nine canoes. The lake we enter was once an ancient river. Since it has been dammed, the river's shape has become a long lake with fingers of land reaching into the water. Does the river object to having her shape changed by the will of some humans who make it their business to do such things? The lake is silent on this matter. We never think to ask such questions. The water level is lowered during the summer months leaving stretches of smooth, white sand populated with the skeletons of white driftwood tree trunks in various poses. We pitch our tents on these welcoming shores.

Over the course of several days, we paddle through veils of mist, past dark islands to the marshy end of the lake. The feeling is one of going deeper, back into an earlier time. Despite the human-made changes there is no evidence of our species, no reminders, just the pleasant green smell of being near the mouth of the lake that once was a river. We have come here to immerse ourselves in nature, to listen to our dreams, to become a tribe of women who travel by canoe, sleep in tents, swim naked in the lake. We go to recover from our busy lives and remember ourselves. Other than paying our fee, we do not ask permission to be here. We don't know who to ask.

Anne and I have taken women to this place for several summers. This particular trip is arduous. The weather is hard, a strong north wind makes choppy waves on the lake. Paddling takes effort. The group is choppy, too, filled with factions, tensions, friction. The dreams we dream at night and gather during the day are ominous, full of argument, weather, big winds, storms, betrayal, and, dare I say, something deeper. As dream-tender, I feel concern and know we are opening a conversation about the darkness that lives within us and around us.

At sunrise Anne sends her voice out in an echoing chant and we gather for our morning meditation. Two deer swim across the lake heading for our tents. When they register the sound, the strange shapes and the presence of two-footeds on their shore, they startle and swim back to the other side of the lake. I don't like this, the feeling we have intruded, pitched our tents in their living room. Uninvited guests. That night I have the distinct sensation that someone is trying to suffocate me. I wake up in a heart pounding panic.

In the morning we take our tents down and prepare to move our camp. We wade in the water and load our canoes. In the shallows, our bare feet touch bones. Many bones. We reach into the lake bottom and pick them up—thigh bones, femurs, knuckle and hoof bones. Like little kids on a treasure hunt, these bones excite us. A few of us take them as souvenirs. The ominous feeling from the night before remains with me although I, too, against my own nature, pick up several knucklebones. We determine these bones probably belong to deer or moose. They are not old, but not fresh either. That night at the far end of the lake, the sky reddens and gives the water a skin of blood.

Early the next morning we gather in a circle for our meditation. In the distance the sound of a lone motorboat can be heard as it toils up the lake in our direction—an unusual sound as this lake is usually vacated by late August. We intentionally pick this time for our journey. We never see or hear people much less people in boats with motors. Whoever is in the boat is looking for us. When the boat reaches the sandy shore Anne and I go to meet the man to see what he might want—to tell us we are illegally camping? to warn us of something? We recognize him from the country store where we paid our fees and put our canoes in a week ago. He is visibly upset. In a low voice he tells us that the son of one of the women on the trip has been killed in a car crash.

We absorb the shock of this news. Tears spontaneously run down our cheeks. We walk back to the circle of waiting women, dreading the task ahead. We kneel next to the woman and tell her the news that is every mother's nightmare: "Your child is dead. He has been killed in a car crash. We don't know anything else. Your husband is on his way." Women cry out; we hold the woman whose tragedy this is; she is in terrible shock. We help her pack and I agree to accompany her on the long trip back down the lake where her husband is waiting.

The man in the motorboat takes us. The wind has made the lake treacherous and the metal boat pounds hard against the whitecaps. It is a jarring, teeth-rattling, heartbreaking journey. The woman's long, white hair goes wild in the wind and she is raving, unable to fit herself into an impossible reality. She cries into the wind, "We don't belong here! We should never have touched those bones!" She is mad, a female Lear, and, I think, maybe she is right.

The man in the motorboat drops the woman off to the waiting husband and takes me back to the campsite. Upon my return, I find our fractious group deeply bonded, petty differences forgotten in the face of a sudden death of a child.

The next day we paddle down the lake heading toward home. I am carrying a driftwood doll that the woman handed to me at the last minute before she left with her husband. I am spooked by it. It feels uncanny, like a fetish loaded with danger. The group energy shifts as we head towards home. The women become self-oriented, eager to return to the comfort and security of homes and loved ones. They want distance from the frantic tragedy that melded them into a community of mourning women. I do, too.

I return home carrying my gear, some moose bones, a rattle that I picked up at our final giveaway, and the driftwood doll. I enter the house and Jim welcomes me. I tell him what has transpired; I show him the moose bones. He looks at me and says, "There are spirits of the dead all around you." This is not his usual way of talking. But the minute he speaks these words I feel seen, my fatigue understood, my hovering spirit grounded. I ask, "What should I do?"

We piece together a makeshift ceremony, open all the doors to our house, sweep the spirits gently out with a broom, and sprinkle a trail of cornmeal outside for them to follow. Then we smudge the house and each other. I place the moose bones, the rattle, and the driftwood doll out on the back deck. But that night I tell him it would be better if we did not sleep together in the same bed. He agrees and goes upstairs to sleep in his study.

In the middle of the night, I dream that I am in my room in bed when I hear a loud rattle being shaken close to my ear, followed by a long, piercing human cry. Then someone is shaking me so hard that my teeth chatter. Terrified, I try to call out. I wake up in a sweat with my heart pounding.

In the morning, I quickly wrap the driftwood doll in a box and send it back to the woman who made it. I take the give-away rattle and the moose bones and drive to a swampy area. Jim tells me that some people think it best to take uncanny things to a place where people are not likely to walk. I step through some tall grasses and hunker down at the edge of the marshy water and ask the swamp to receive these things and transform them. A very large green frog watches as I dispatch the things into the swampy water. I do not think to ask the frog's permission to rid myself of what I don't want into his home.

Once I am relieved of these artifacts, I feel there are two more things I must do: go to the Maine State Museum and research this particular lake and the ancient people that once lived there, and second, return to the lake and make peace in some way with the spirits of that place.

The Maine State Museum houses a large diorama of Lake Aziscohos, which was once a river. I learn that over 10,000 years ago Paleo-Indians ventured up this river for summer hunting with flint spears brought from farther south. Archaic Indians who followed them 7,000 to 5,000 years ago as the tundra was being replaced by pine forests, hunted caribou with spears and fished with harpoons and hafted hooks. Do the spirits of those ancestors still live on the land I wonder? Do they care about how the land is being used and exploited? Or have they been washed from human memory by all the many passing millennia? Has the power of red ochre, which signaled the presence of the Red Paint People, been bleached out of our present-day consciousness? On the map, I notice that the place where we camped, the middle campsite where we found the bones in the water, was once the site of the Paleo-Indian people's big hunt. The deer or moose bones we found were not ancient, nor were they fresh, so was finding them in that place a matter of coincidence?

I also learn that paper companies have heavily logged here, leaving a forested edge as a so-called "beauty strip," creating an illusion of the once thickly treed forest; that low-flying planes carrying poisonous weed-killers spray the trees and all the creatures that have their homes here; that engineers dammed the river; the once plentiful animals have disappeared, many species exterminated. This place of the great hunt is no longer honored as a sacred, food-giving site. We have severed our primal connection with this land, the animals, and the people who once inhabited it. In our inarticulate need, we have gone there in hopes of finding what has been so lost. The woman's words come back to me; "We don't belong here." And I suspect that in her madness she speaks the truth. At the very least, we should have asked the questions that Barry Lopez (2020) recommends when he approaches an unfamiliar landscape. "Who are you? How do I say your name? May I sit down? Should I go now?"

Even after many months, I am hounded, dogged by whatever had shaken me in the night. I catch glimpses of something out of the corner of my eye; I have intrusive thoughts, particularly when I drive; I fall off the back edge of my deck, or was I pushed? I feel in danger. It takes almost a year to resynchronize my life.

Jim and I make a trip to the lake in October. The trees are ablaze and their vivid colors are perfectly reflected in the flat mirror of lake water. I go alone to the water's edge where I cry out to the silent waters. I ask for permission to sit down, I want instruction. From what I can sense, the spirits want honoring, and they want food. This was their hunting ground, their place of food gathering. Of course they want food. I know it was hopelessly naïve of us to go to their place on a Dreamquest without addressing the spirits of these first peoples and the animals who once lived on this land, without acknowledging their history and that of the lake that was once a river. I make an offering of food and ask forgiveness. I enter a place of deep stillness within myself and wait.

References

Sachs, N. (2011). "The Chorus of the Stones." In N. Sachs, *Collected Poems 1944-1949*. Trans. M. Hamburger, R. & M. Mead, & M. Roloff. Green Integer.

Lopez, B. (2020). "Love in a Time of Terror: On Natural Landscapes, Metaphorical Living, and Warlpiri Identity." *Literary Hub*.

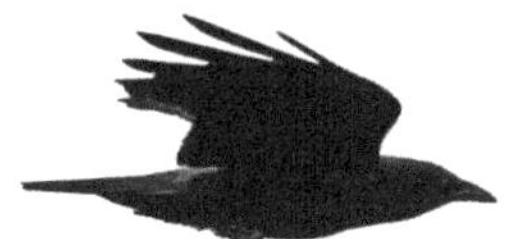

Regan Holt

Rendering the "Reinhabitation"[1]

amiskwaciy wâskahikan[2]

is a place name
quaking
the landscape
spirit

a valley occupied by beavers
in the Aspens hills
gather

a big sky river
cascades over
glacier conditions

weathering
sparkling
flowing

[1] *Reinhabitation*, according to bioregional scholars Peter Berg and Raymond Dassman (1990), is defined as "learning to live-in-place in an area that has been disrupted or injured through … exploitation" (p. 35).

[2] amiskwaciy wâskahikan is the Cree-nêhiyawêwin place name for Edmonton, Alberta, Canada, meaning *beaver hills house* (Donald, 2004; LeClaire et al., 1998; Shields et al., 2019). Notably, the Cree language, or nêhiyawêwin dialect here, does not use capitalization conventions for proper nouns. According to local scholars Kyle Napier and Lana Whiskeyjack (2021), this dialect avoids the practice of capitalization conventions prevalent in English grammar "so as not to hold orthographic hierarchy and prioritize one word, sound, or morpheme as more important than others" (p. 3).

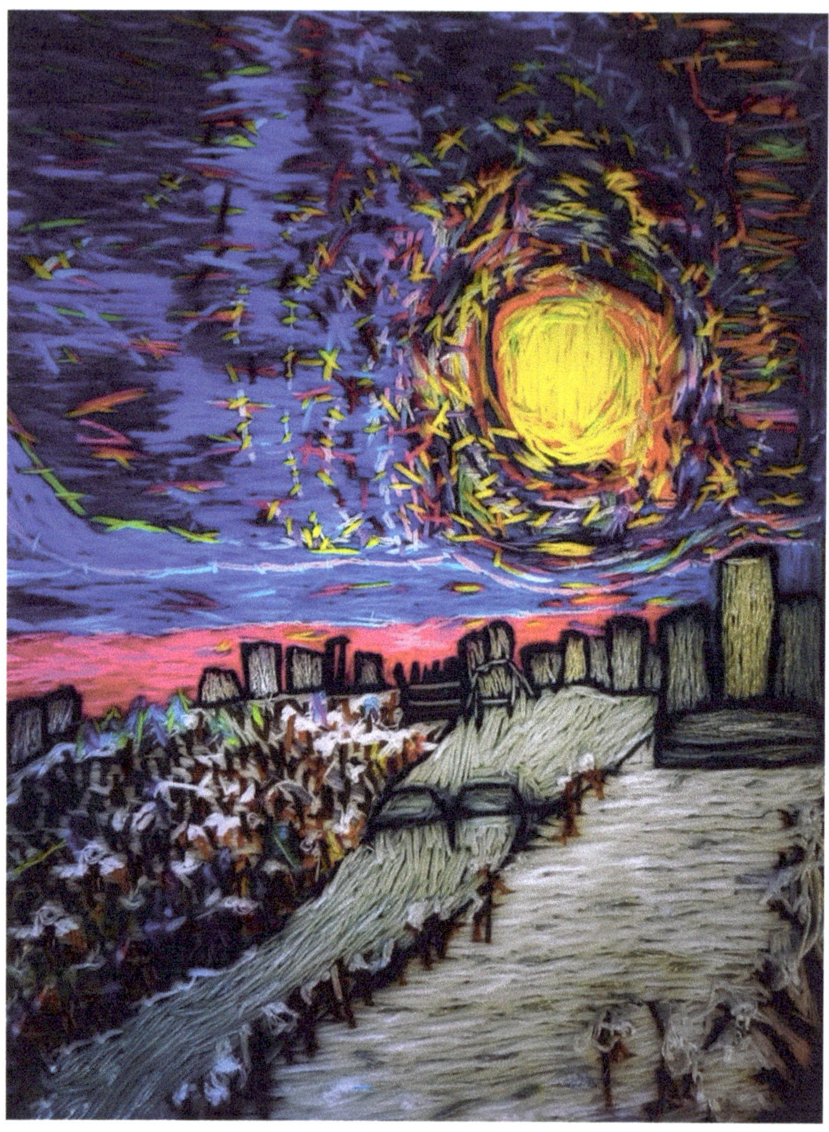

Edmonton, Alberta, March 8, 2022. amiskwaciy wâskahikan. [Embroidered with acrylic floss in and through a white plastic backing stabilizer using a yarn darner, framed, and filtered using the Snapseed application for Android devices; by Regan Holt].

under quilted clouds
busy birdsong echoes
coyotes tiptoe the embankments

watery reflections
ripple on through
dividing
shades of the season

too soon snow frozen
the land and river blanches
winter storms
white-out

despite all the frostiness, the sun does shine.

References

Berg, P., & Dassman, R. (1990). Reinhabiting California. In C. Plant, V. Andruss, & E. Wright (Eds.), *Home! A bioregional reader* (pp. 35-38). New Society Publishers.

Donald, D. T. (2004). Edmonton pentimento re-reading history in the case of the Papaschase Cree. *Journal of the Canadian Association for Curriculum Studies*, *2*(1), 21-54. https://jcacs.journals.yorku.ca/index.php/jcacs/issue/view/713

LeClaire, N., & Cardinal, G. (1998). In E. Waugh (Ed.), *Alberta Elders' Cree Dictionary/alperta ohci kehtehayak nehiyaw otwestamâkewasinahikan* (p. 4). University of Alberta Press.

Napier, K., & Whiskeyjack, L. (2021). wahkotowin: Reconnecting to the spirit of nêhiyawêwin (Cree Language). *Engaged Scholar Journal: Community-Engaged Research, Teaching and Learning*, *7*(1), 1-24. https://doi.org/10.15402/esj.v7i1.69979

Shields, R., Moran, K., & Gillespie, D. (2020). Edmonton, amiskwaciy wâskahikan, and a Papaschase suburb for Settlers. *The Canadian Geographer/Le Géographe canadien*, *64*(1), 105-119. https://doi.org/10.1111/cag.12562

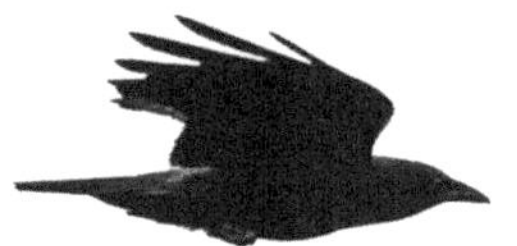

Christi Kramer

Tracks//Light

She took from her pocket all she gathered in the wood, burdock bur and root; fireweed, sap and gum, to make the world, to make the world well.

A word, to soften the wounds of the injured, she read.

This has been the way I've known to attend. The spells I've carried. My whole life I've moved from the urgent given that, "the whole of the world must prevail" (Bringhurst 2008, p. 43). Forgiveness; reach; trace: it has always been poetry. Home: this magical garden, we are. I've loved it. Many people have thought themselves at the end of the world. We wriggle with our mortality; dust the house to prove our being before the unsettling; *from dust we are to dust we shall. Return* has been the theme of all my longing.

What will you do? There will be no one to lead you.

If there is no river, no ibis or chora
If there is no whisper which way

No pontiff, mother, shaman
There will be no drum, no waving prayer to guide you

No horizon, no stupa, no star
No piece of bark or beach of sand to crawl into

No moss or rock or garden
So how then, will you walk foot before foot to your heaven? (Kramer, 2012, p. 85).

We do not know what it is to *not exist.* This is the awe that embraces me now. Could it be that my son was born at the end of the human world? Perhaps the whole will *not* prevail. There very well may be *no one* to pick up the traces that we are. Less courage; I did not notice that the singing could only be for now alone. The ego had hoped for a future, I suppose. My grief sings here to all we were. Nostalgia does give place for dreams.

There was a time humanity stood in the winter field and sang into the night

Some in their houses ran to blow out what cast on the window light.
whisper—fat deer in belly-snow search grass; tail and leap

bark   and the palm of the hand   held stars
we once were

If, in yonder time you should read

we once were.

It was that in the winter we made tracks:
mice, deer, our son's, my own.

It was epic, life; we were in awe.
"All the natural movements of the soul are controlled by laws analogous to those of physical gravity. Grace is the only exception. [....] Two forces rule the universe: light and gravity. [....] Grace is the law of the descending movement. [....] fall toward the heights."

— Simone Weil, *Gravity and Grace*, 1997

Kneel I down right now to you mycelium; O tiny white flower; cedars, under you neck bent, we whirled; sky, you always there and faithful; that languages died, is true. "There is gonna be another extinction," said my five-year-old son born at the end of us, our world; left to you, the smallest (wee bacterium), flourish in your rich decomposing. "Mommy, which organ don't we need?"

I heard a poet say that the landscape, this particular, forest, *Beloved, longs* for me.
If only I had lived that way. Who will miss us and how? No one to say even, this was the foundation, where the tornado had passed, where once a house.
mud bottom of the marshes take a deeper breath

fern, dragonfly and sturgeon
it is
returned to you again.

Imagine we turned into light.

It doesn't matter that there was a ladder here. The human moved in her yard.
As did the hummingbird and squirrel. She imagined if her planet had become something else, this planet, be it fern again or burbot, luminous unknown, another might dwell
A mound of layered debris, what we called a *tell;* a heap, like a breast
what we breathed out, piled. The names for places they lived: Levant, Anatolia, Ur, this small hill: home

We were a people who planted beets, from pokey seeds to pluck and pickle.
Our discussions were, without theatrics, of how the open mouth which often sang in praise, would receive the earth with silent hallelujah on that day. The calling of the black-capped chickadee. The goshawk in circle a sky beyond ears also now what will be the holders of dirt and gentle worm. What was a reaching back of generations

why she was thrown each time to her knees at the smell of earth, what drew her down; cell memory of another's bowing; blessed mycelium; blessed
what was

Here was the track,
where once was the child,
who with a stick,
turned over the carcass of a fawn.

The rib cage—the Sistine Chapel—
what he carried forever with him since

not just the question of touch
and God

Once, when all these *made in the image* walked through cedar, brushed by bows
there was the distance
Once, there was the distance

and thus the reach

for dramatic effect, to be read as the voices of Gregorio Allegri: *Miserere*
(the unrecorded version)

We were people who told stories of dragons and salvation; of children lost, found; of pots that filled and filled eternally to match hunger. Such concern there was for pebbles strewn, for paths abandoned; for the hearth, the lintel, the plow, violin and bow.
There were etchings in wood, metal, stone. Glass, you may know, returns easily to sand. Still, there were many who combed the beach, that is walked slowly; toes as intimate with the shore as Magdalen with her lover's feet. There was, lest we forget to speak of it, an anointing, yes. And reverence.

Should you find small green or blue or amber chips—what the sea wore smooth,
There were also hands—proof this did exist.

It was like this; you may have been just at your kitchen table; or stirring soup;
or at the loom, amidst the carded wool and lanolin; maybe you were otherwise engaged
but it is almost certain you stopped, almost; to listen

There were among us, those who sang their wares
pots for sale, precious milk; onions, radish, silk There were those who sang
give me your ruins, your broken things and I will turn them for you
again
there was the turning. and those who sought the ruined place
the hovel of their own making

Things like this went on. If you can imagine
a pause at the window sill

And all the while the singers and the sellers passing.

We swam from as under as our lungs would carry us to a surface of light and shimmer, here, we may have felt ourselves light; exhaled into our new becoming.

"The present was an egg laid by the past that had the future inside its shell."
—Zora Neale Hurston, 1939

There was a poet who said,

"There will be no other end of the world."
—Czeslaw Milosz, 1988

You would have understood us, were you to have read such a poem.
There were, in fact, many poems. A tended garden; plowed notes; the poets' grief—or something like grief—(if there is anything like grief). So many opinions and a wave that pulls you under. That the poem sailed in some way toward the direction of their longing; that is to say, the people nuzzled notions that could not be said, gnawed at them. but the poets did their best. and if, by chance, you read . . . . we were more than one thing at once

those tomatoes
ripe or green

left on the vine to hang
There were those who sought to bring on the end; fretted about the color of the heifer's hair, a red calf; happy little creature pulled at mother's tit; tripped as all toddlers do, through hay and muck. There were those who gathered arms; (not held gathered in each other's arms), but named the guns and bombs that aimed; stocked larders and dug bunker; bent wire around their own; *scales and scrolls and horsemen; famine, pestilence and plague*, some people said. It is true there was a red horse. There was a girl in the corner of the room, who drew a horse and painted it red. She drew a calf too; the only color pencil her sister didn't take with her to school. Even the barn, of course, was red. It is true too, that there were cellars full of apricots preserved, the garden
harvest taken in before frost; all of this the people had learned, how to prepare for the quiet of winter. a celebration each night by the fire.
There were those who burst into other houses, opened and unleashed their fear.
There was a pale horse and a sword.

We built spaces you could enter, where a voice in song trembled walls.
There was something you may know: silence. We often missed it
but not always. There was a thing called music built around it. Beams held up the structure; clay, mortar and pigments. We tried. The Cappella Magna;
niche of marble for sacrament. Oh, yes, we had ceremony. Except for when we forgot.

One of our favorite things to do was place a morsel in the lover's mouth. Perhaps, every single one of us knew this, the desire to feed and be fed.

Some children died along the side of the road

So much could be said; so little. (*until it didn't matter*) There were those who told stories of floods; doors locked and fists banging the boat. There were boats overturned. There was a young man who sailed an inner tube with hope for a better shore. There was hope; people had hope. There was the beauty of the sun on the wave. We beheld beauty, and sometimes we did not. Sometimes one person shot a hole into another's raft and said, *you do not belong among us. Us*, is a notion we people had. Always there was the clinging, the grasp to remain afloat
We liked to buy and sell and trade, almost everything: shiny glass beads, the world; things we stitched and carved; and a whole slew of make believe, numbers and such. There was one who liked to place apples in a bucket. There were five she counted, as she dropped each in took it out. Sometimes the bruise is worth it. There were things we enjoyed even more after the peeling away. Set a pie in a window—practical if no crow, yet cliche. Yes, we decided some things we had had enough of. For those who had it, dessert staled in a few days. There was a ping and thud in the bucket. That is what she liked most, the repeat. We imagined, as much as we tasted, the sweet.

If you notice how the vines move, verdant granadilla grasps her tendrils, grip and cling; we were like this. O for an object to hold onto, the pull into another. to place ourselves, grow. We had a telescope we called the *bring 'em near,* meaning the stars. Every single one of us sparkled, brilliant in our desire for the pinholes by which we steered.

So we should not be flung
Even in our reaching up, we were most at home with gravity to weigh us down.

We divided the day; followed shadows, water, the clepsydra, used floats and scales; melted wax; sifted sand; measured mercury; hung true pendulums. We soldered; tuned quartz oscillators; balanced springs; coordinated universal time. Before this, there were sticks, stones, the moon. Always, we counted, begged for more. We were larger when the sun was behind us. What was cast, falling bodies.

If you see a scar, wealled it strip mine, clear cut, dominion. We had our breakfast of coffee with milk (easy, I woke to tea and soy). O Amazon. All of it was given to us *to subdue, to rule.* We called it ours. We were gatherers of honey; held the comb between our teeth and sucked smoke and clover. We made cookies, unwrapped chocolate from foil; made rubble and crumb. There were those who beat drums, loved and protected the water. We were, for the most part, water. Our tears rained down on us and we drank them in.

Labyrinth, aqueduct, cradle, pen

References

Bringhurst, R. (2008). *The tree of meaning: Language, mind and ecology.* Counter Point.

Hurston, Z. N. (1939) *Moses, man of the mountain* (p. 99). J. B. Lippincott Co.

Kramer, C. (2012). "Return." In J. Currin, J. Hall, R. Hsu, C. Leclerc, N. Reimer, M. Sawatsky, & D. Zomparelli (Eds.), *The enpipe line: 70,000+ kilometres of poetry written in resistance to the enbridge northern gateway pipelines proposal* (p. 85). Creek Stone Press.

Milosz, C. (1988). "A Song on the End of the World," The collected poems 1931-1987 (p. 7). HarperCollins.

Weil, S. (1997). *Gravity and grace* (pp. 45-48). (Trans, A. Willis) University of Nebraska. Original publication 1952

Kate McGabe

I stand
  at the water's edge
  waves licking my toes
  my soles made tender.

I remember
  sand, water, and wind.

I realize the Earth has been holding me gently all along.

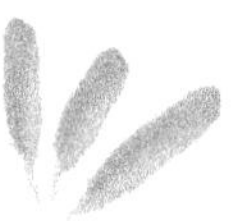

McGabe, K. (2022). Found poem from Gasp. Struggle. Let go. In A. Fidyk, & D. St. Georges (Eds.), Poetic Inquiry for synchrony & love: A new order of gravity [Special Issue]. *Art|Research International: A Transdisciplinary Journal*, *7*(2), 458-476.

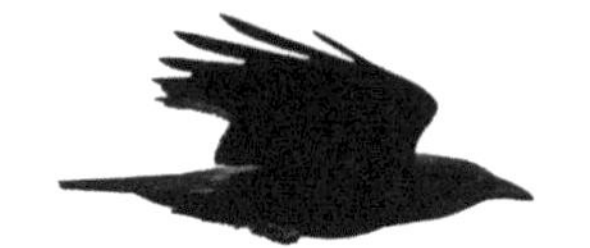

Adriana Oniță

Proverbe românes ți potrivite pentru orice ocazie / ***Romanian proverbs for any occasion***

Have you ever considered the gravity of losing your mother tongue—the sacred first language you loved and were loved in? When I close my eyes, I wonder if I will ever speak Romanian again as fluently as I did when I was a child. I wonder if fiul meu will learn it as his mother tongue. I think about ironia vieţii mele: how I have made a living by teaching other languages—Spanish, Italian, French, English—colonial languages with gravitational fields, languages people desire and profit from in a neoliberal world of trade and tourism. Yet, I have never taught my limba maternă to anybody. In fact, I neglected it for a long time (Oniţă, 2022), and for many reasons "s-a ascuns. It disappeared inside / corpul meu, my body's weight / and I know it's still there" (Oniţă, 2019). Dar, am început să mă întreb: How might I honour my familial and ancestral wisdom through my poetic practice? The emotional and spiritual pull towards limba maternă led me to compose this work based on Romanian proverbs. I wanted to carry over precious pieces of wisdom that I frequently heard growing up from my mother, my aunts, and my grandmother. Here you can savour proverbs and pictures that act as curatives—for catastrophic times, for disillusionment, for doing and undoing, for gravity, for love, for synchrony, and for being responsible to our art.

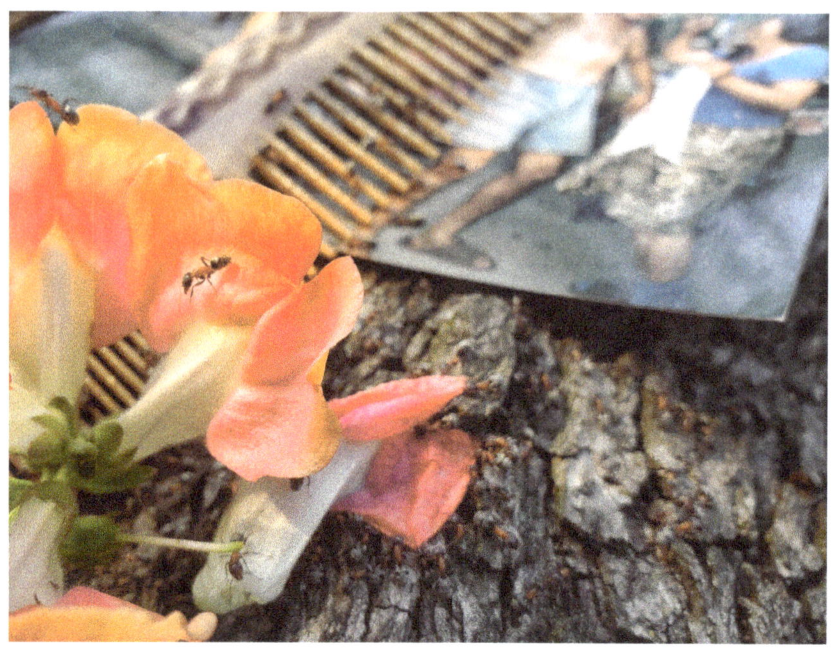

Țara arde și baba se piaptănă.
The country is burning and the old woman is brushing her hair.

Cine seamănă vântul culege furtună.
Whoever sows the wind reaps the storm.

Colac peste pupăză.
Braided bread on top of a hoopoe (misfortune never comes alone).

Punem țara la cale.
We'll put the country on track (we'll gossip and solve nothing).

Fă haz de necaz.
Laugh through your woes.

Fă-te frate cu dracul până treci puntea.
Make the devil your brother—until you cross the bridge

La plăcinte înainte, la război înapoi.
Head to the pies, leave war behind.

Și tăcerea e un răspuns.
Even silence is an answer.

Înţeleptul tace și face.
The wise work and don't talk.

Grăbește-te încet.
Hurry slowly.

Poate să ningă, poate să plouă; am canadiană nouă.
It can snow, it can rain; I have a new Canadian jacket.

Apa trece, pietrele rămân.
Water flows, rocks remain.

Pentru deziluzie / *For disillusionment*

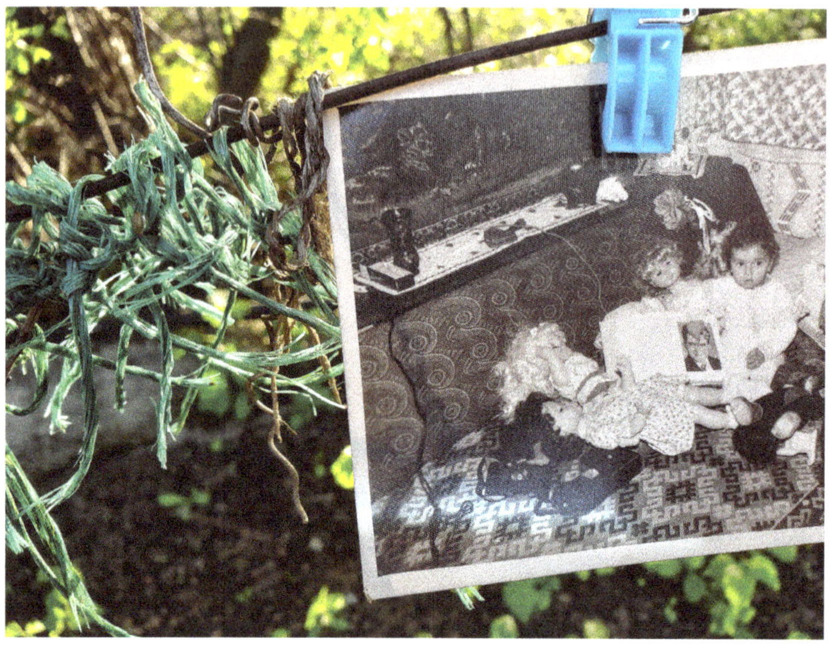

Mănânci un sac de sare cu un om și tot nu-l cunoști.
You can eat a sack of salt with someone and still not know them.

A fost prins cu cioara vopsită.
He was caught with a painted crow.

Mincinosul roade osul.
The liar gnaws at the bone.

Câinele care latră nu mușcă.
A barking dog never bites.

De departe trandafir, de aproape borș cu știr.
From afar, a rose, and from up close – borsh with amaranth grain.

Cu o floare nu se face primăvară.
One flower does not equal spring.

Aceeaşi Mărie cu altă pălărie.
Same Maria, different hat.

Ce-i lipsește chelului? Tichie de mărgăritar.
What does the bald man need? A pearl hat.

A arătat pumnul sub batistă.
He showed a fist under his handkerchief.

Grăbește-te încet.
Hurry slowly.

Pentru a face și desface / *For doing and undoing*

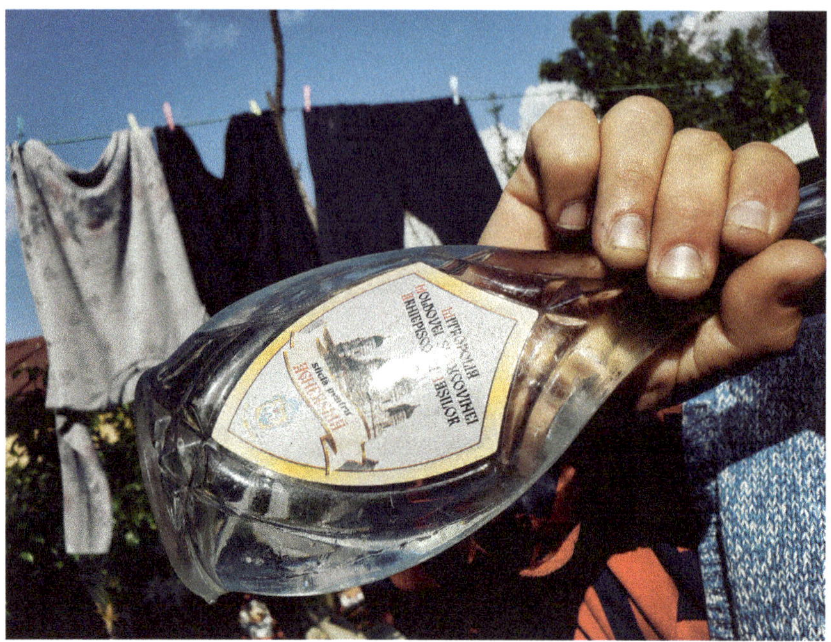

Am împăcat capra cu varza.
I reconciled the goat with the cabbage.

Câini latră, ursul merge, noi muncim cu spor.
Dogs bark, a bear walks, we work hard (we pretend to work).

Fă rai din ce ai.
Make heaven from what you've got.

Grăbește-te încet.
Hurry slowly.

Am cărat apă la fântână.
I carried water to the well.

Vrei, nu vrei, bea, Grigore, agheasmă!
Gregory, whether you want to or not, drink the holy water!

După mine, potopul!
After me, the flood!

Pentru gravitate / *For gravity*

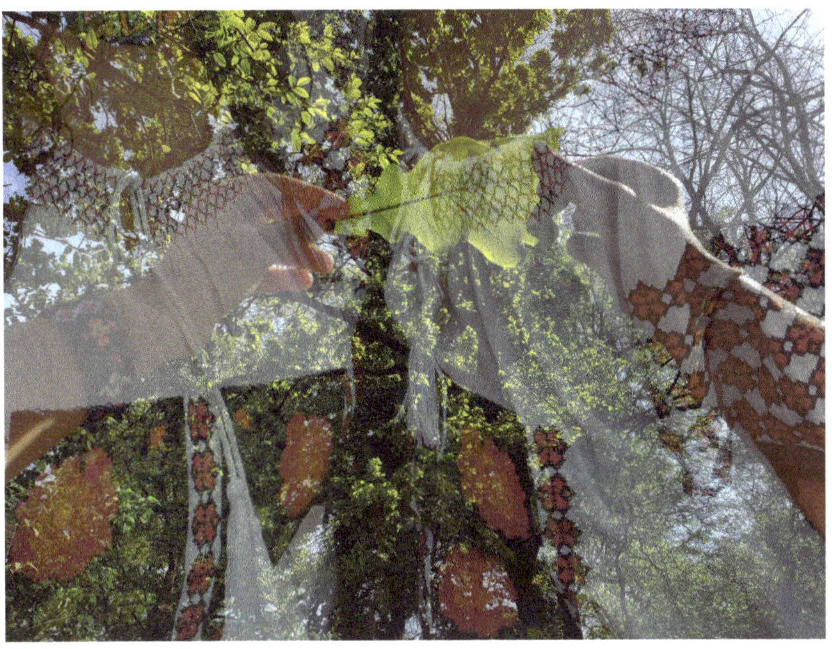

Celui înțelept îi ajunge un cuvânt.
One word is enough for the wise.

Cine are carte, are parte.
She who has a book has power.

Din stejar, stejar răsare.
From oak, oak rises.

Găina bătrână face ciorbă bună—dacă morcovul e tânăr!
Old hens make good soup—if the carrot is young!

Câinele bătrân nu latră degeaba.
Old dogs don't bark without reason.

Vulpea bătrână ocolește capcana.
Old foxes avoid the trap.

Grăbește-te încet.
Hurry slowly.

Celui înțelept îi ajunge un cuvânt.
One word is enough for the wise.

Pentru iubire / *For love*

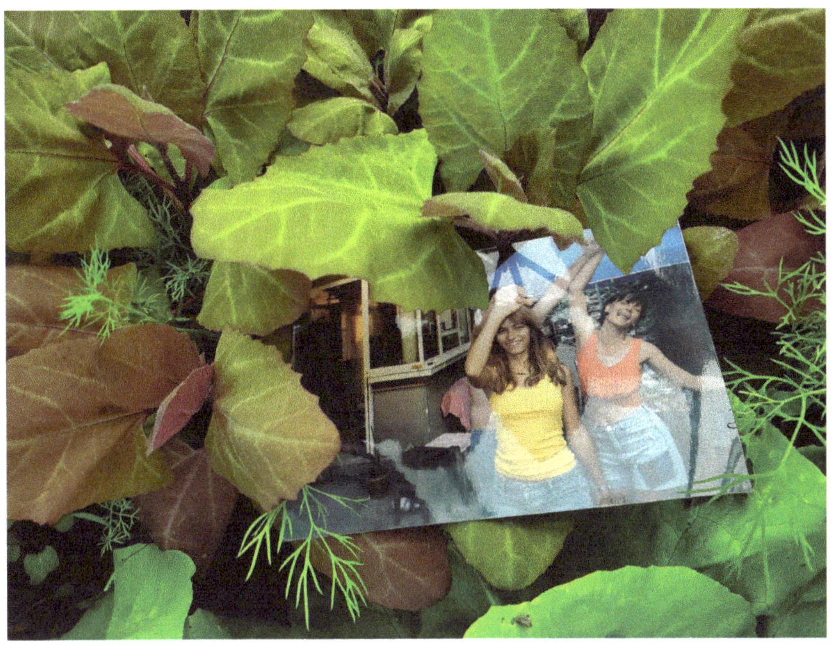

Cu răbdarea treci și marea.
With patience, you can cross the sea.

Grăbește-te încet.
Hurry slowly.

Vorba lungă, sărăcia omului.
Too many words make us poor.

Vorba dulce mult aduce.
Sweet words will get you far.

Dragostea cea veche îți șoptește la ureche.
Old loves whisper in your ear.

Foaie verde lobodă, gura lumii-i slobodă.
Green orach leaf, the world will always run its mouth.

Laudă-mă gură, că ți-oi da friptură.
Praise me, mouth, and I'll give you steak.

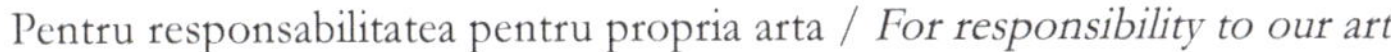

Pentru responsabilitatea pentru propria arta / *For responsibility to our art*

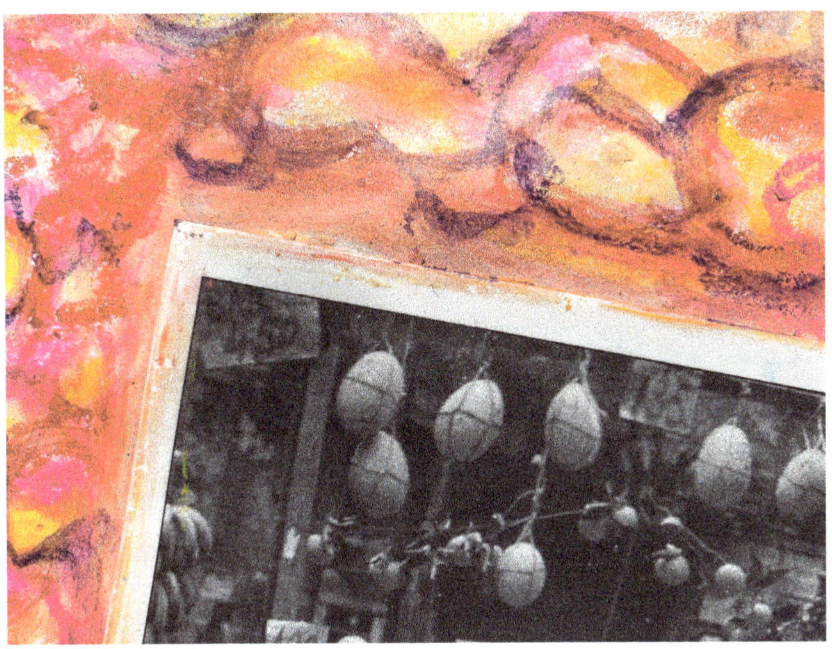

Brânză bună în burduf de câine.
Good cheese in a dog's bellows (don't waste your talents).

Ești ca cimbrul, în toate.
You're like thyme, in everything (involved in too many tasks).

Omul gospodar face vara sanie și iarna car.
If you're wise you make a sleigh in the summer and a wagon in winter.

Omul harnic, silitor, de pâine nu duce dor.
A hardworking person can't go hungry.

Hărnicia întrece arta.

Diligence surpasses art.
Munca sfințește locul.
Work makes our space sacred.

Graba strică treaba.
Rush ruins work.

Grăbește-te încet.
Hurry slowly.

Ai intrat în horă, trebuie să joci.
You entered the horă, so you have to dance.

Pentru sincronie / *For synchrony*

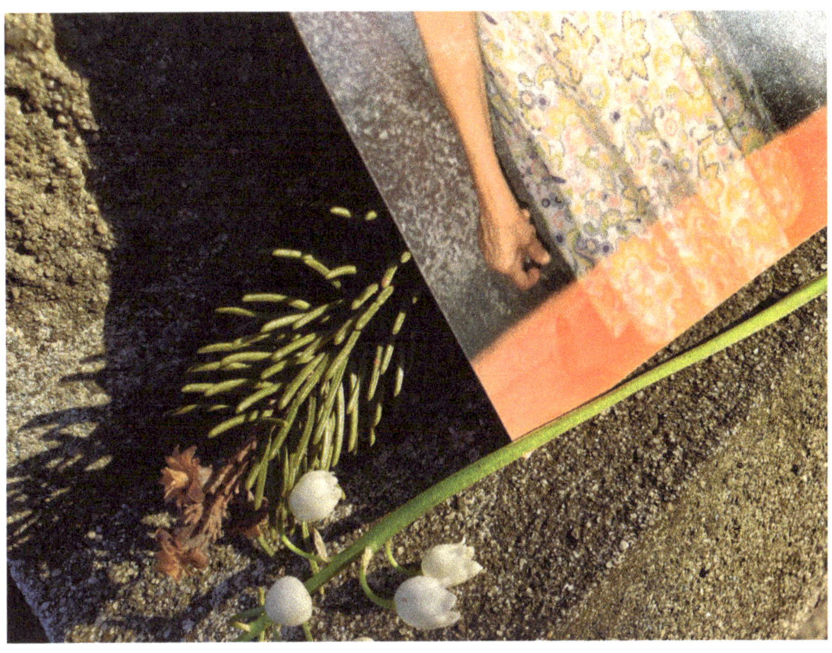

Nu te lupta cu morile de vânt.
Don't fight the windmills.

Grăbește-te încet.
Hurry slowly.

Dacă vântul nu suflă în pânze, vâslește.
If the wind doesn't blow in your sails, paddle.

Tragi nădejde ca ursul de coadă.
You're hoping too much; it's like pulling a bear's tail.

Cine se aseamănă, se adună.
Birds of a feather flock together.

Ce ți-e scris în frunte ți-e pus.
Your fate is written on your forehead.
Don't fight the windmills.

Grăbește-te încet.
Hurry slowly.

Dacă vântul nu suflă în pânze, vâslește.
If the wind doesn't blow in your sails, paddle.

Tragi nădejde ca ursul de coadă.
You're hoping too much; it's like pulling a bear's tail.

Ce ţi-e scris în frunte ţi-e pus.
Your fate is written on your forehead.

Images

Oniţă, A. (2022). *Țara arde și baba se piaptănă.* Digital photograph.
Oniţă, A. (2022). *A fost prins cu cioara vopsită.* Digital photograph.
Oniţă, A. (2022). *Vrei, nu vrei, bea, Grigore, agheazmă!* Digital photograph.
Oniţă, A. (2022). *Din ștejar, ștejar răsare.* Digital photograph.
Oniţă, A. (2022). *Foaie verde lobodă, gura lumii-i slobodă.* Digital photograph.
Oniţă, A. (2022). *Grăbește-te încet.* Digital photograph.
Oniţă, A. (2022). *Brânză bună în burduf de câine.* Digital photograph.

References

Oniţă, A. (2022). *Arts-based curricula for heritage language development and maintenance.* [Unpublished doctoral dissertation]. University of Alberta. https://doi.org/10.7939/r3-njpw-zp09

Oniţă, A. (2019). Limba maternă: A creative inquiry into mother language shift and loss. *In:cite Journal, 2*(1), 51-57. https://doi.org/10.33137/incite.2.32820

Alexandra Fidyk

Our Love is a Prayer

Our love is a prayer
years pleated, bent back
folds disguise

sadness tucked
along the edge
laughter on the short-end.

Dense fibre weaves
run horizontal, trace
time across the realms

ancestral lines, raven-
inked, karmic script.
Prayer is our love.

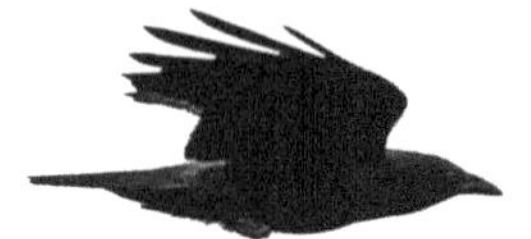

Jodi Latremouille

Grandpa Lou, at 88
would bounce Gertie on his knee
and sometimes spank her lightly
on her big round bum
"You granny," he would say
and she beamed like he had just handed her
a dozen red roses
but of course, roses
were frivolous,
"bah, humbug,"
you know

one day he fainted at the kitchen table
on Thanksgiving
the whole family leaped into action
instantly converging on our collective silent denial
I was at his head when he came to
"You kid," he said as he lay on the floor
and I wiped my unruly, humbug tears
discreetly on my sleeve

the pacemaker bought a few years
but Grandpa Lou slowed down, mellowed out, smoothed over
he let us kiss his bald, freckled head
with only a hint of that disapproving frown
slightly marred by a tiny sly upturn
at the corner of his tired mouth
"You rats," he would call us grandkids
and we would beam like he had just brought out

Gertie's famous crystal bowl of stale,
hardened candies

his twisted, knotty hands
taught us to play crib and fix fences
he presided over our woodwork projects
and baseball games
catching our tiniest mistakes with his foggy, sharp blue eyes
he never let us forget that we could never
do anything
say anything
make anything
right
"I'm no use to anyone," he said one summer day
After a fender bender in the parking lot
The final day before the day that he decided
his driving days were done
sometimes it got too loud at family gatherings
he would just smile
and nod
"Is that so?" he would say
we could finally say no wrong
when he turned his hearing aid off
that was usually right before he nodded
off to sleep
slumped over
sitting upright in his chair

that night in the hospital room
he couldn't bring himself to make amends
but he was too weak to growl
when I silently rubbed the shoulders
of the tired, withered
version of him as a tall young man
"You angel," he said
and I knew that I had
finally gotten one thing right

Lauren Levesque

I cannot move the constellations brightening the evening sky
I know even as I breathe, the sea may break these ties

. . . acts of love and rebellion as slow time

Levesque, L. (2022). Found poem from Small sounds in familiar places: A Poetic-visual inquiry on the gravity and synchrony of love in pandemic times. In A. Fidyk, & D. St. Georges (Eds.), Poetic Inquiry for synchrony & love: A new order of gravity [Special Issue]. *Art|Research International: A Transdisciplinary Journal, 7*(2), 327-350.

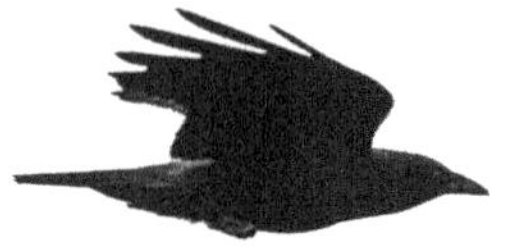

Nicole Rallis

Walking with Eros

I invite you, dear readers, to sit with my musings on eros as a way to linger with animate ontologies: to sense the aliveness of the present moment, to challenge structures that see the world in a moribund state, and to embrace the relational and emergent nature of our existence that is at its base, love. As a settler Canadian of mixed European descent who lives and learns on traditional and unceded territories, it feels impossible to think about animacy and love for the land, each other, and the more-than-human world without also considering the ongoing violences of colonialism. I share with you a snapshot of my ongoing poetic walking practices along the dormant Esquimalt and Nanaimo (E&N) Railway tracks near my home in Shawnigan Lake, British Columbia, the traditional lands and waters of the Quw'utsun peoples. My practice which I call *walking with eros,* is a poetic inquiry that investigates and resists colonialism to walk with the land embracing an "All My Relations"[3] worldview. These poetic walking practices have helped inform my dissertation research, where I also walk alongside an array of art-educators (poets, dancers, painters, sculptors and musicians) in the Cowichan Valley to learn how they engage the lands they love, teach and create with to think through ecological and cultural issues.

In Canada, important calls to action outlined by the Truth and Reconciliation Commission of Canada (TRC, 2015) and the National Inquiry on Missing and Murdered Indigenous Women and Girls (MMIWG, 2019) ask us to question our

3. "All My Relations" is an important phrase used across several Indigenous cultures on Turtle Island (North America) to express the interconnectedness of all creation (people, animals, plants, land, sky, waters). Thomas King states that, ""all my relations" is an encouragement for us to accept the responsibilities we have within this universal family by living our lives in a harmonious and moral manner . . ." (1990, ix).

relationship with the land and existing structures that perpetuate ongoing violences toward Indigenous communities and the natural world. Most recently, the discovery of mass child gravesites at several former residential schools has heightened the need for educators to reflect on the violences within colonial educational systems (Tk'emlups te Secwepec, 2021). There have been recent institutional acknowledgements and commitments to reconciliation through education guided by the TRC. In British Columbia, the province where I reside, public schools are embedding the First Peoples Principles of Learning into curriculum (BC, 2022). The core principles state that "Learning is holistic, reflexive, reflective, experiential, and relational (focused on connectedness, on reciprocal relationships, and a sense of place)" (n.p.). Despite commitments to reconciliation through education, Ray, Cormier and Desmoulins (2019) note that there is still "a real need for academics to move toward concrete conversations about the land to significantly reshape settler consciousness" (p. 81).

Challenging colonial frameworks that perpetuate our imbalance with the land and more-than-human world might require the creation of pedagogies and curriculums that, as social work scholar Michele Sorensen notes, "allow for students to enter spaces, conversations and practices driven by calls to ethically and respectfully respond to the violence's of colonialism" (M. Sorensen, personal communication, May 3, 2020). Educators, in particular those of poetic habits of mind and practice, are beginning to realize the magnitude of responsibility they face in re-imagining our world and equipping future generations to think more holistically and justly. To re-imagine the world, we need poetic practices to help provoke dialogue and challenging discussions. We need poetic practices to develop deeper relational understandings of our love for the world. I walk with humility—knowing that I cannot aptly capture the complexities of each idea I poetically engage with—and also with playfulness. To walk with eros is to embrace the beauty and potentials of the unknown and emergent. I offer my writing as a gesture toward and an invitation for educators to think about all their relations by exploring ideas on matter, animacy and reciprocity that are guided and grounded with love and care.

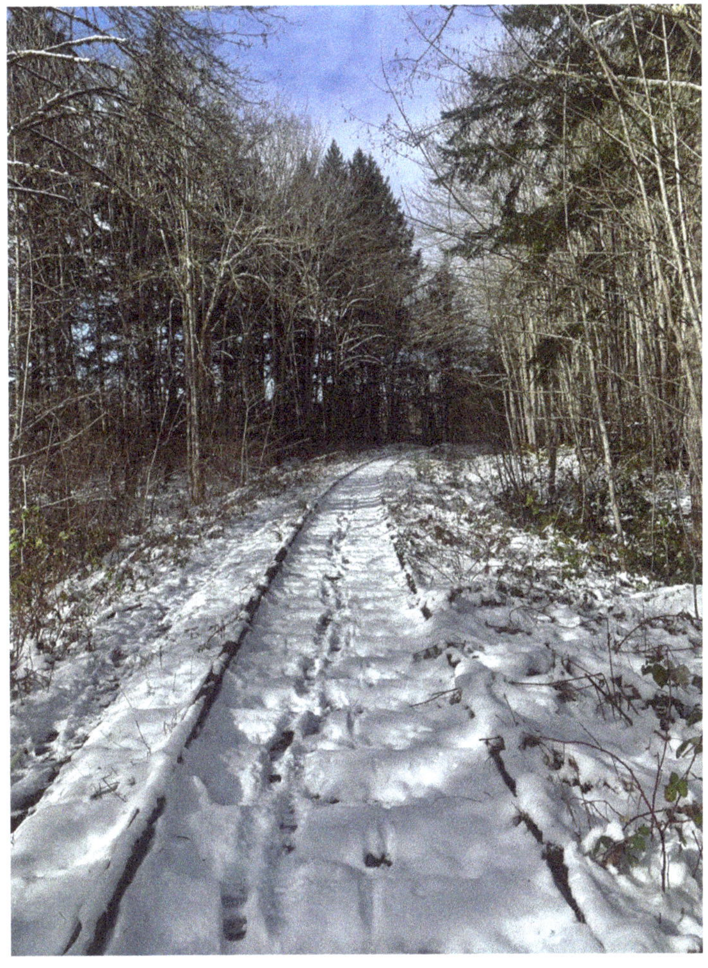

Tracks on tracks, 2021. Photo credit: Nicole Rallis.

Walk #1

onto the train tracks
a pink winter sunset
shivery crunchy sounds

tiny paw prints line the steel rails
tracks on tracks

now my tracks add
stuck in my head

where
who
what
is eros

how can eros lead the way

For many educated in the West, theorizing about love often emerges from an encounter with Greek philosophy. In *The Symposium*, Plato (1999; 285 BCE) tells a story of a great feast where speeches are given in praise of Eros. Eros is both recognized as erotic love and as a phenomenon capable of inspiring wisdom, truth, mortality, and goodness. At the feast, Socrates describes a conversation he had with the prophetess Diotima. Diotima speaks of Eros not as a God, but as a spirit that is halfway between God and man. She believes that spirits are "intermediate between the other two, they fill the gap between them, and enable the universe to form an interconnected whole" (Plato, 1999, p. 39). She tells Socrates about Eros' birth from the god Resource and the deity Poverty. Diotima asks Socrates why is it that love is always that of beautiful things. She reveals that beauty is not the end but the means to something greater, the achievement of a certain production of birth: "Love's function is giving birth in beauty both in body and in mind" (p. 43).

As I engage with Plato, I also look to other educators with poetic tendencies who have lingered with eros. I collect their words and create a cento.[4]

sorE

the genuine principle of life
uniting earth and sky
making humans so round
once united they cannot be defeated.

[4] From the Latin word for "patchwork," the cento (or collage poem) is a poetic form composed entirely of lines from poems by other poets.

why is the world so beautiful
an erotic ecology
of gravity
intimacy and connectedness
permeating
worlds of bodies
words in love
sow

the great magician

There are many connections between how educators poetically engage with eros and how animate ontologies, cosmologies, and worldviews are taken up in the work of botanist and enrolled member of the Citizen Potawatomi Nation, Robin Wall Kimmerer (2003, 2013, 2020). In Kimmerer's writing about plants, she speaks about the grammar of animacy, the Earth's animacy, and paying deep attention to the aliveness of the natural world. She reminds us that Western science has largely ignored the grammar of animacy. In a podcast interview with Krista Tippet, Kimmerer tells the story of how she engages her university students to embrace the erotic and how seeing the world as alive and relational brings a heightened sense of responsibility to learners:

> In talking with my environment students, they wholeheartedly agree that they love the Earth. But when I ask them the question, "Does the Earth love you back?" there is a great deal of hesitation . . . . It's a really liberating idea to think that the Earth could love us back, but it also opens the notion of reciprocity that with that love and regard from the Earth comes a real deep responsibility (Tippet, 2020).

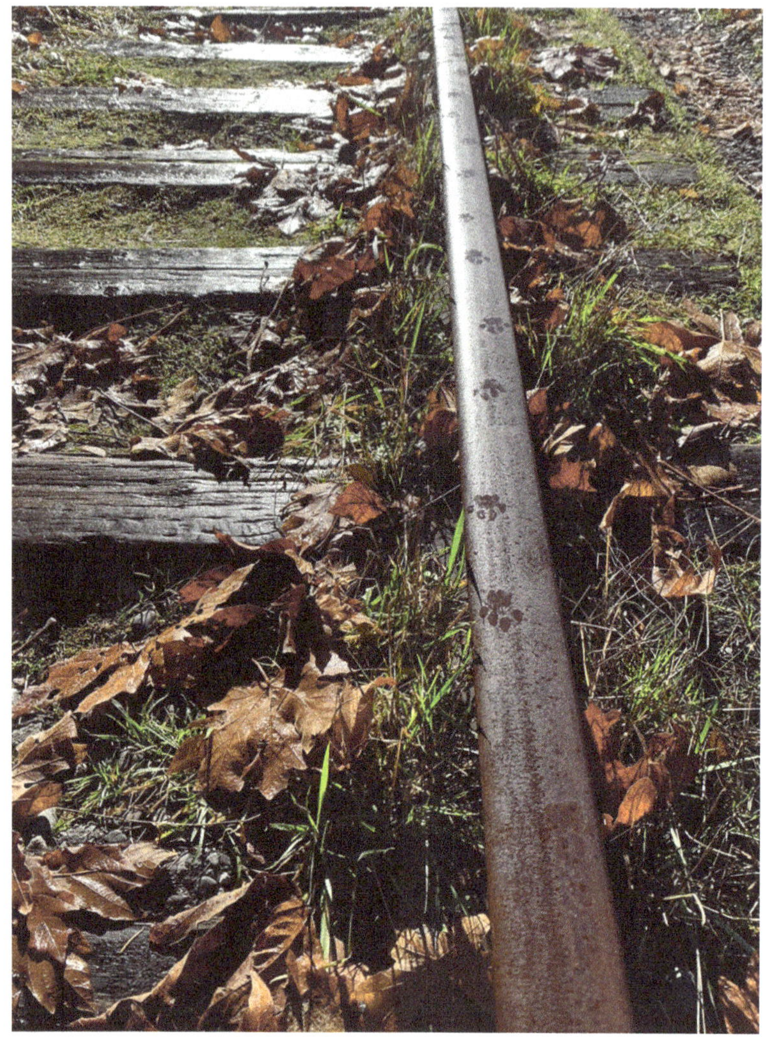

Noticing, 2021. Photo credit: Nicole Rallis.

Walk #2

back tracking
onto the tracks
again
walking differently

re-tracing steps
embracing the unknown

taking response-ability
relationally with animate and inanimate
the world feels softer and tougher
at once

embracing animacy
is also recognizing
the ghosts that haunt these tracks
tracks of a past and present
taking of land

Walking on the dormant tracks that figuratively and materially leave a reminder of colonial violences of the past on the land and with the traditional stewards of these lands, push me to find balance—to hold the past and present in suspension and to continue to look out for ghosts that linger. Stephanie Springgay states that "decolonization [in education] must attend to inherited ghosts that are alive and ongoing, but which can also be imagined otherwise" (2021, p. 31). Walking with eros is one way in which I poetically engage with what can be imagined otherwise. Opening up to love—for the land, each other, and the more-than-human world—awakens within me a new somatic response-ability.

Dear readers, I would like to share some questions to linger with. *What can we notice when we walk (and create) with eros? How does eros help attune us to the animacy of the land and more-than-human world? Moreover- how can eros help us engage in caring and reciprocal relationships?* Eros calls on us to be embodied learners and to practice and live with an ethics of care (Harney & Moten, 2021). I am also reminded of the crucial questions posited to me by one of my committee members and mentors, "*How does the body get on the page?*" and "*How is the pencil writing me*?" (P. Cole, personal communication, June 22, 2021). I carry these questions with me and pay attention to how I am made and re-made through my waking/creating /writing with eros. When I write, create, and walk with eros, it is in relation to the authors I have read, the conversations I have with friends and family, and paying attention to the plant, animal, water, sky, and tree teachers I come across on my walks. Walking with eros is a continual and intentional asking for the consent to relate and the consent to be in relation with. It is a daily reminder that teaching and learning are loving and communal acts. Thank you for coming with me on this journey.

breaking from

we are living through the sixth mass extinction
losing sight of our heart and our spirit
upholding the mind and the (scientific) eye
over

embodied ways
intuitive ways
a-rational ways
of being

how do we nurture
curriculums that allow us to grieve
remembering and restoring
a balance of and with *all our relations*

many have written about the power (and magic) of words
transforming
informing
creating worldviews

power   full
creation
trickster
sacred   stories

colonialism
not a monolithic structure
a set of contemporary and evolving

land relations
maintained by good intentions and even good deeds[5]

docility
white fragility
histories buried
distorted truths

we forgot
the original instructions
living with spirit
the spirit world is more real than most of us believe

object
thing
it   detachment
rationality

nouns
labels
categories
reductionist

static   thought   (s)

trapped in mind
in grammar
syntax
wanting   heart   spirit   lifeforce

nature
the natural order
requires animacy
verbing

5. The italicized parts of this poem are inspired by the words of Kimmerer, 2013, Liboiron, 2021, and Westermann, 2007.

what comes first
language or worldview
maybe neither
story ourselves into being

storytellers remind us
land
comes
first

warnings
signs of degradation
the loss of words (language)
and how we treat and teach our children

mechanic
static (statistical)
indoor screen time
textbook(ed)

subjective (subject)
progress(ive) or regressing
no more full sentences
only relational matter

potential to unlearn and relearn
to be in tune (re-tune)
restoring balance with the more-than-human
if you speak it ...they will hear you

running the course
layered and complex
built upon sediment
histories & erasures

layers intertwined
bodies and land intimately connected
remembering
                    the circle is never closed

References

Betasamosake, S. L. (2014). Land as pedagogy: Nishnaabeg intelligence and rebellious transformation. *Decolonization: Indigeneity, Education & Society*, *33*(3), 1-25.

Harney, S., & Morten, F. (July 2, 2021). *The aesthetics of abolition, the abolition of art* [video file]. YouTube.https://www.youtube.com/watch?v=TyilsdXlgl8&ab_channel=FondazioneGramsciEmilia-Romagna

Kimmerer, R. W. (2013). *Braiding sweetgrass: Indigenous wisdom, scientific knowledge, and the teachings of plants.* Milkweed Editions.

Kimmerer, R. W. (2003). *Gathering moss.* Oregon State University Press.

King, T. (Ed.). (1990). *All my relations: An anthology of contemporary Canadian fiction.* McClelland and Stewart.

Liboiron, M. (2021). *Pollution is colonialism.* Duke University Press.

National Inquiry into Missing and Murdered Indigenous Women and Girls. (2019). Reclaiming power and place: The final report of the National Inquiry into Missing and Murdered Indigenous Women and Girls. https://www.mmiwg-ffada.ca/final-report/

Plato. (1999). *Penguin classics: The symposium.* Penguin Books.

Province of British Columbia. (2021, October 11). *First Peoples Principles of Learning* [Press release]. https://www2.gov.bc.ca/assets/gov/education/kindergarten-to-grade-12/teach/teaching-tools/aboriginal-education/principles_of_learning.pdf

Ray, L., Cormier, P., & Desmoulins, L. (2019). Fish fry as praxis: Exploring land as a nexus for reconciliation in research. In S. Wilson, A. V. Breen, & L. Dupre (Eds.), *Research & reconciliation: Unsettling ways of knowing through Indigenous relationships* (pp. 73-85). Canadian Scholars.

Springgay, S. (2021). Reconciliation and education: Artistic actions and critical conversations, In B. Vivienne, Z. Michalinos, M. Siddique, & H. Dorothee (Eds.), *Higher education hauntologies: Living with ghosts for a justice-to-come* (pp. 88-101). Routledge.

Tk'emlups te Secwepec. (2021, May 27). *Office of the chief: For immediate release* [Press release]. https://tkemlups.ca/wp-content/uploads/05-May-27-2021-TteS-MEDIA-RELEASE.pdf

Tippet, K. (2020, August 20). *Robin Wall Kimmerer: The intelligence of plants* [Audio Podcast]. On Being. https://onbeing.org/programs/robin-wall-kimmerer-the-intelligence-of-plants/

Truth and Reconciliation Commission of Canada. (2015). *Truth and Reconciliation Commission of Canada Final Report.* Winnipeg: Truth and Reconciliation of Canada.

Westerman, F. R. C. (2007, September 4). Indigenous Native American prophecy (Elder speaks) [Video file]. http://www.youtube.com/watch?v==g7cylfQtkDg

Annette Wentworth

On the Lyrical Lament

> To compose (*poiein*) ourselves in the face of the many distractions represents one of the great and *healing* promises of engagement in poetic inquiry, whether as researcher, writer or reader. Examples of this sort of "unknowing" work, of the kinds of thought and writing that might come of it are . . . lively, life-giving . . . . (Seidel, 2017, p. 157)

I've been attending to the AIDS pandemic in Africa for nearly fifteen years. This means I live with ghosts, I invoke them, and my writing and research reflects this particular haunting. Because I am a literary writer and thinker (Woudstra, 2007), my scholarly inquiries are often written in a way that also reflects this way of thinking-being. And as my topic demands from me an embodied response, my writing lives close to the bone.

As Lorri Neilsen (2008) points out: "our researching selves seek the language that best creates intimate and ethical connections with one another" (p. 94). So, I reach out a hand; I offer a lyrical lament, lines ringing with the particularities of pain and loss.

One of the fundamental questions of my research is inspired by Roger Simon's work on remembrance and the pedagogical possibilities of learning to live with loss. Simon asks us to consider "what it might mean to take the memories of others (memories formed in other times and spaces) into our lives and so live as though the lives of others mattered" (2005, p. 9)? What does it mean, for me, in the context of my experiences of the AIDS pandemic in South Africa? How do I live? Alongside the dead, the diseased, the disconsolate, and the defiant—I only know how to dwell, how to pay attention, how to howl, and how to sing.

Writing or telling (or sing-storytelling, lyric writing) a detailed and embodied story, and evoking sensory images, is one answer to Simon's question. It has the possibility to heal—both the writer and the reader (MacCurdy, 2000; Seidel, 2017). Because trauma and painful memories and experiences are embedded in non-verbal areas of the brain, powerful poetic writing can cut through the "story of the story" (MacCurdy, 2000, p. 166) we often tell to shield ourselves from being returned to trauma. To take the other into our lives and to make them matter, we need all our senses, and we need story.

I heard, saw, and felt a story that changed my life when I attended the XVI International AIDS Conference in Toronto in 2006. It told a detailed, embodied—embroidered—tale of loss, and of courage. On one of the arts-based evenings at the conference, I went to the St. James Cathedral and heard a woman from the village of Hamburg, in the Eastern Cape of South Africa, introduce the Keiskamma Altarpiece. Amidst singing and tears, the Altarpiece was opened to reveal its inner panels. I was simply astounded by its size, artistry, and story. I was shaken awake, again, as one is over and over again in life, to an entirely new set of possibilities and astonishments.

That day in 2006, my life and this enormous tapestry-textile work collided, and I felt all the possibilities of art—to address suffering, and resistance, and loss. Maybe these were keys to unlocking the indifference to others I find so distressing: keys to unlocking the doors of the mind and heart. Here were threads that weaved the suffering of humanity throughout the centuries into a solidarity of sorts; into the acceptance of sorrow with the longing for social justice. A leap into the fray—the fraying edges of these woven pieces that tell and show us what it is to be alive, to live alongside, and to wonder; loose threads aching to be tied to one another and stitched into something stronger.

I became tied to this community in South Africa, suturing myself into the scenery so artfully described by the women of the Keiskamma Art Project[6] who created the Altarpiece (Wentworth, 2021). The scope of the AIDS crisis in this community,

6. The Keiskamma Art Project, is the initial group of women that began in 2005 in a rural village in the Eastern Cape of South Africa and grew into a multifaceted community organization: the Keiskamma Trust. See https://keiskammaartproject.org for the history of the art project and to see more of their work.

where I ended up living and working for nearly seven years, (and where I still have a home today), was staggering. The disease, on top of endemic poverty, unemployment, transgenerational and intergenerational trauma and violence, was devastating. What I witnessed living and working with this community continues to haunt me and has worked its way into my academic endeavors since I returned to Canada. That experience continues to inform my research, skew my perspectives, and fuels my desire to find ways to attend to this time and place and the people who are mostly ignored, not only by the international community, but also by their country as a whole (Thomas, 2014).

This is why I lament, through lyrical poetic writing, to story, explore, and bear witness to the effects of the AIDS epidemic in South Africa. I embrace the ambiguities that are allowed—even encouraged—by a lyric inquiry or lament. Poetic language is full of fragments, of gestures that acknowledge language as always inadequate, as it most certainly is, for reflecting the faces of the millions who died of this disease, and of those whom it desolated.

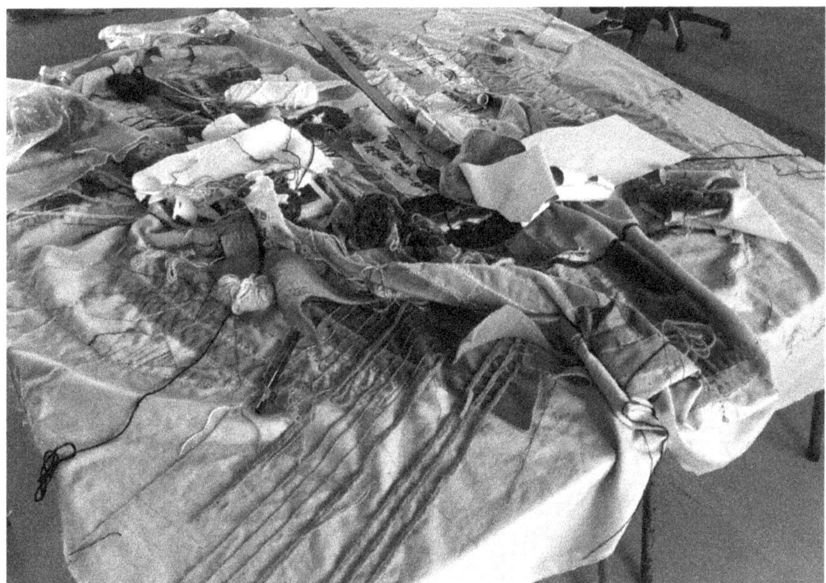

Entangled[7]

7. The Keiskamma Art Project, beginning a tapestry, 2017, photograph supplied by author.

The South African poet, Ingrid de Kok, in her poem "Mending" (2006) writes,

> In and out, behind, across.
> The formal gesture binds the cloth.
> The stitchery's a surgeon's rhyme,
> a Chinese stamp, a pantomime
>
> of print. Then spoor. Then trail of red.
> Scabs rise, stigmata from the thread.
> A cotton chronicle congealed.
> A histogram of welts and weals.

My lyrical lament aims to stich in similar ways, binding stories together in poetic writing, against the stigma and the scabs, to trail my own lines of red, to follow and to find memory. Poetic writing and thinking listens with a hermeneutic ear which is attentive, in-depth, welcoming, and engaged. It engenders humility and lives in service to the questions that my time in South Africa and my connection to that community continue to ask.

This kind of poetic writing is also deeply intuitive (Neilsen, 2008; Moules, McCaffrey, Field & Laing, 2015) and respectful of each particular person, place, event, circumstance, and embraces—even insists on—recognizing that all of these come with their own deep history and individual languages (Jardine, 1998). To write with resonance, towards an understanding, albeit fleeting and temporary, is also to be in love with language, which I have been all my life. Language is also the way I love and live in the world, even as I lament.

Poetic, lyrical and hermeneutic writing, Moules (2002) writes, is the practice of opening what was once closed, unearthing what was hidden. It is a "process by which things emerge from concealment into unconcealement" (Moules, 2002). This is what I hope to do in my re-searching life: uncover and attend to a time and place and people who are over-looked, disregarded.

Poetic inquiry pays attention, it listens with love that does not wish to own or to contain. It works against colonizing or Western-European categorizing practices that have for so long dictated the terms of life and of death for others (Siedel, 2017). Instead, poetic or lyric inquiry imagines without appropriation, ownership or reductiveness (Neilsen, 2008). Lyric inquiry eschews power, it contemplates, it admits defeat and embraces unknowing.

Poetic knowing/unknowing and being allows for a felt sense or body response, it wants to dwell in experiences and language and material, it feels the weight of the cloth and the sting of a stitch gone-awry—the unexpected needling.

Lyric inquiry "invokes justice and tells the truth even when it hurts. It aligns itself with the brokenhearted and the ones who suffer. It teaches how to live wisely and heals with compassion. It bows to...those whose names we do not know—all those early beings, our kin, who are now leaving or already gone from this world . . . . Penultimate grief" (Seidel, 2017, p. 154).

Dis-ease, or ill-at-ease: to research along the lines of loss, to contemplate an ethical way to witness the AIDS pandemic in South Africa. However, to be disconsolate may also allow for the impossible possibilities of hope, because in the dissonance room is made for new responses, new—always contingent—meanings, and the imagination of something other and better to be made, together.

> In lyric, nothing is accidental: if a detail fits into a composition, the possibly of this fitting must be written into the detail itself" We can imagine any given detail—any identifiable part of a lyric composition—as a set of possibilities of resonance, some of which are actuated by situation the detail in the context of the composition.
>
> (Zwicky, 2011, p. 114)

Every stitch, every story counts, it fits— it must fit—"you *must* have it both ways: the immediate preciousness of each individual thing and the coherence of the whole" (Zwicky, 2011, p. 111). I take this to heart, yes, we must have it both—all—ways. Always. Come back, into life, into living memory, into re-memberance, all of you dear ones that have fallen away or are under the earth. The whole must be made up—it can only be made up—if all of you are in it.

Come dying, diseased, disconsolate ones. Come all the enraged and the reeling. Come with delight, come with dirge, welcome into the song, for all of us are part of the singing.

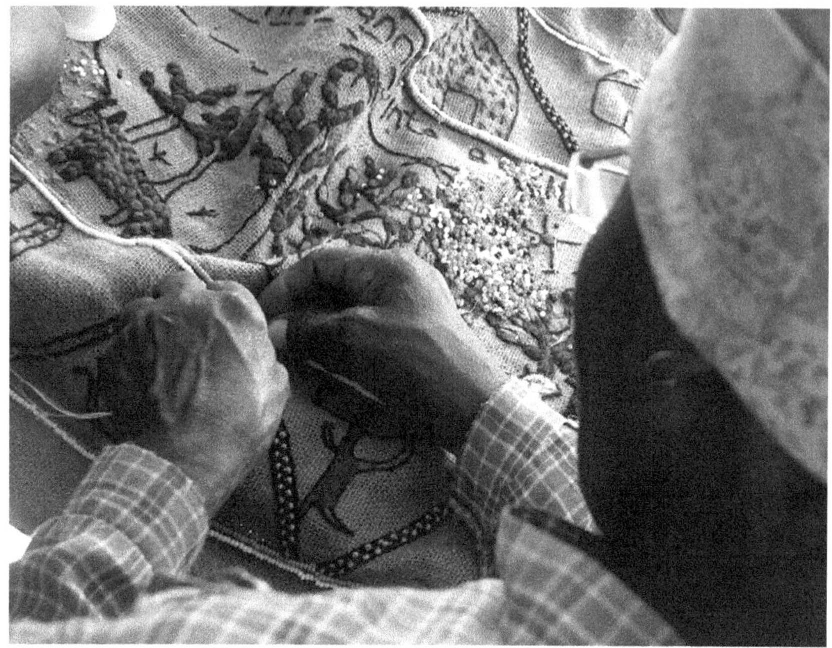

Keiskamma Tapestry[8]

(The final stanza in Ingrid de Kok's poem "Mending" (1997)):

> The woman plies her ancient art.
> Her needle sutures as it darts,
> scoring, scripting, scarring, stitching,
> the invisible mending of the heart.

8. Photograph by Robert Hofmeyr, 2003, used with permission of the Keiskamma Trust.

References

de Kok, I. (1997). "Mending," from the book *Transfer,* found in *Seasonal fires: New and selected poems* (p. 72). Seven Stories Press.

Jardine, D. (1998). The fecundity of the individual case: consideration s of the pedagogical heart of interpretive work. In D. Jardine, *To dwell with a boundless heart: Essays in curriculum theory, hermeneutics, and the ecological imagination* (pp. 34-51). Peter Lang.

MacCurdy, M. (2000). From trauma to writing: A theoretical model for practical use. In C. Anderson, & M. MacCurdy (Eds.), *Writing & healing: Toward an informed practice* (pp. 158-200). National Council of Teachers of English.

Moules, N. (2002). Hermeneutic inquiry: Paying heed to history and Hermes, an ancestral, substantive, and methodological tale. *International Journal of Qualitative Methods, 1*(2), 1-21.

Neilsen, L. (2008). Lyric inquiry. In J. G. Knowles & A. L. Cole (Eds), *The handbook of the arts in qualitative research: Perspectives, methodologies, examples and issues* (pp. 93-103). Sage Publications.

Seidel, J. (2017). Poetic inquiry as unknowing. In L. Butler-Kisber, J. Guiney Yallop, M. Stewart, & S. Weibe (Eds.), *Poetic inquiries of reflection and renewal: Poetry as research* (pp. 153-161). MacIntyre Purcell Publishing.

Simon, R. (2005). *The touch of the past: Remembrance, learning and ethics.* Palgrave MacMillan.

Thomas, K. (2014). *Impossible mourning: HIV/AIDS and visuality after apartheid.* Bucknell.

Woudstra, A. S. (2007). *The green heart of the tree: Essays and notes on a time in Africa.* University of Alberta Press.

Zwicky, J. (2011). *Lyric philosophy.* Gaspereau Press.

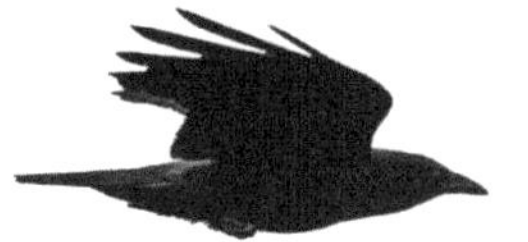

Maya T. Borhani

Living poetically is both ethos and praxis,
poetry embodied in our beings and actions
in tune with the oneness of all things

Orbital revolution of planets around sun,
satellites around planets
planets around axes
overlapping, intertwining celestial bodies
the way of synchronicity

I grow quiet, return to listening, pay deeper attention,
embody love even in grief and despair.

Borhani, M. T. (2022). Found poem from Tracing paths of love through poetic inquiry. In A. Fidyk, & D. St. Georges (Eds.), Poetic Inquiry for synchrony & love: A new order of gravity [Special Issue]. *Art|Research International: A Transdisciplinary Journal, 7*(2), 497-518.

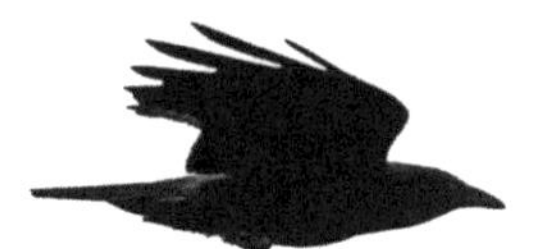

Crystal Andrushko & Yulit Price

This morning a sourdough was given to me[9]

Price to Andrushko

her hands unraveled the striped
black and white towel gently cradling it/
sour   rustic   round/
the sound of scoring scribed/
around the crown//

it started with a starter/
it started
with idontknowhow/
it started with volition
to make something come alive/
just when life was shutting down/
it started
with making herself come alive/
instead of giving up//

I play god and cut a slice of life/the knife
gliding on the surface/ the butter
warming   into
the empty   wanting   holes//

I can feel her and I and bread and butter
and what started us all   all moving with aliveness//

9. The following are excerpts taken from a collection of letters exchanged between two poets, which belong to a collaborative project called: "Letters to a Credible Friend."

Embrace

Andrushko to Price

This poetry refuge we share fillsthe empty wanting holes in me.
I hold your sourdough gift in my imaginary hands,
smell it, listen to you speak it into life.
Life.
All my life I wanted to enter poetry with someone
who
could hear me   and here you are.
Wild improbability of our melding spirit in the centre
of wintered city, in an old schoolhouse covered in *papier mâché.*
You: the prized gift in the *piñata* I finally bought from the market stall
where a small man generates a warm smile. Warm like sourdough.
Warm like the world of our poems. Warm like the body.

What poetry does

Price to Andrushko

isn't that what poetry does to us?
leave us gasping for air and coming back for more?
I too didn't know how to start or where to enter
but the *piñata* inside?   I knew.
it was bursting with forgotten goods reaching their due date.
You: are the playmate, the throbbing heart, the thumping bat bashing it out of me
I'm taking my turn—
this euphoria of robbing candy from each other, gasping every time it falls out
onto our floor
giddy with gratitude

two female writers

Price to Andrushko

> …it may be enough to cultivate your own artistic garden …. to create alternate worlds that offer both temporary escapes and moments of insight; to open windows in the given world that allow us to see outside it.
>
> —Margaret Atwood

I thought I wanted a love story with poetry
better yet I fell in love with our friendship which surely has just begun yet centuries old

and it feels like at this time—especially at THIS time we live in—that the watering of friendships with words and wonderment IS growing the garden Atwood has asked of us

two female writers in the centre of a story where nothing really happens but poetry
pulled like drunken nectar   pollinating each other
solely for   pleasure
gives me the strength mother earth struggles to offer us now

Oneness with fire

Andrushko to Price

Our room is filled to swell with wonder women
but not a lasso in sight
Pádraig Ó Tuama reads Ada Limón—his tranquil voice and her
goddess words reassure the frozen child in me that she, too, is invincible

Are you also one who swam upstream in pain,
silent and alone?

My teacher said that with acceptance for what we did not choose
arises the compassion to keep going, to see what's true

I want to forgive myself all the failures of kindness
that piled up while I was fighting for my life

The mornings are dark now
My body reaches toward nourishing retreat

poetry makes the news

Price to Andrushko

the news is nonstop weeks away from U.S. election. I pay attention.
amidst the tyranny, unrest, and troubling tension, I seek a place of inner rest.
it calms me to learn Louise Glück has been recognized as a Nobel prize laureate.
her poetry cuts through me quickly. exactly.
isn't it October all over again?
didn't the garden just die?
isn't the pain still in my body? in yours?
didn't we debate the state of earth one more time?

it is cold. we are all afraid to slip on political ice.
there is terror. we have scars.

you planted bulbs for a friend in the ground. I harvest words.
it calms me to write it down.

Countdown

Andrushko to Price

The only poems I write these days are to you,
and from inside
this little nook of being known
The news counts down to the election, but next it will be to Black Friday, to Christmas, to 2021, and then—oh god, will things ever be normal again? Normal: what an ungraspable word.
My best friend counts down the days until we can open our lovemade pickles
I get a text: *14*
then: *3!*
The expectation delights him
I focus on today. I started writing to politicians I didn't vote for. Sometimes they write back.
I reach out so we are wise enough to stick together.
You did a good thing, I say. *This job must be hard. Thank you for caring about us.*
I come home with an armful of peperomias: Schumi red and little fantasy caperatas, clusiifoli jelly, green obtusifolia. It's good to take care of something that needs me.
The gentle politics of plants.

planted here
(or taking from you: "the gentle politics of plants")

Price to Andrushko

Everything is gestation and then bringing forth.
—Rainer Maria Rilke

we gestate in darkness.
seeds in soil—we lean into the land
that surrounds us. germinate in the generosity
of earth's womb offering herself to us:
warm and watered and weighed down
by forces of gravity, and the grave
task of being alive. this being planted here
is a political act. breathing for the first time
on our own. taking in the world's oxygen,
releasing our being in return.
breaking ground. rooting and protruding.
budding into future possibilities

These gifts

Andrushko to Price

I bet you didn't know Rilke and I share a birthday—and it is soon
He showed me how hands can guide a mind out of the dark—and I owe him every word
And maybe too, why my poems long to be a conversation, letters
to a young poet and I keep changing roles
Tiny child with a bellow. Words like sparrow feathers on the wind
You are there in the sky with me, where everything is a gift
Limón and Diaz, too, showed us to frame these ordinary lives
as art—the cold howl of the train beside the river that always reminds me where I live
I love that you still write about plants
even while our days shiver under sheets of cold glass
It's true that the darkness is where truth happens,
and that this world always wants the show
I am not fancy, my peasant blood, perhaps
All my people were poor and worked until they fell back to earth

References

Atwood, M. (2017. Jan 18). "*What Art Under Trump?*" The Nation. https://www.thenation.com/article/archive/what-art-under-trump/

Rilke, R. M. (2016). *Letters to a young poet.* Penguin Classics. https://www.theculturium.com/rainer-maria-rilke-letters-to-a-young-poet/

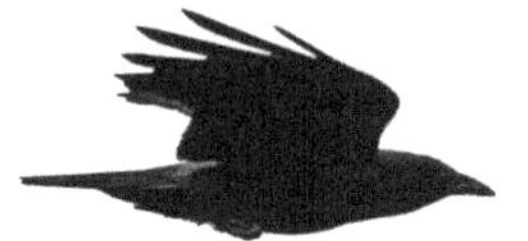

David W. Jardine

Unopened

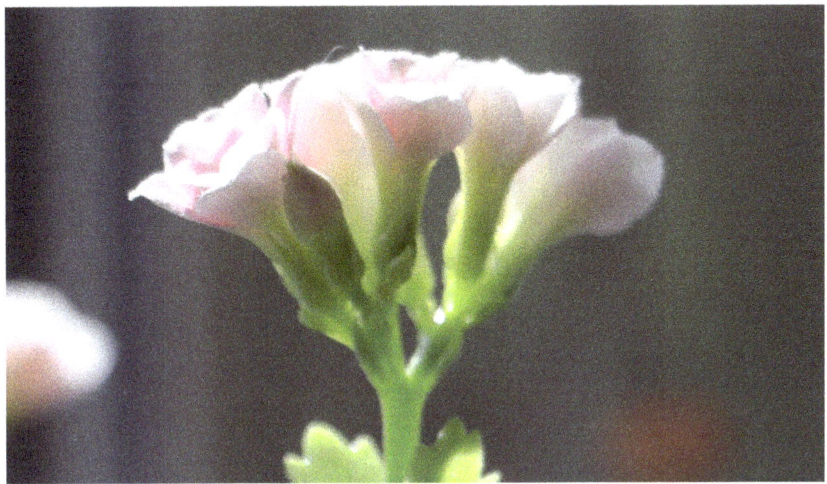

Up.
Close.
There is one yet
Unopened.

There might be a future after all. Always just now opening.
A mighty held for my dying breath. So close.
And oh, the sun feels good as spring comes.
And the son of a son feels good like spring come.
As springs do. For now. And how springs just might do without me.
There's an odd hold, here. A just now
opening. The wood starts splitting.
As does my pain at having done so little to make the open safe and sound.
And the hand I've had in these catastrophic times.

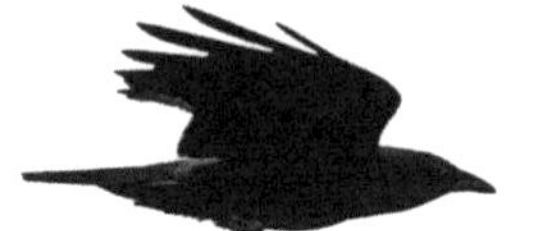

Susan Walsh

heart wind-carved in white

blue prairie cold   crystalline silence
minus 35 degrees celsius   she walks
the ravine so still   crunch of boots on
snow   only her eyes exposed frost on
eyelashes   sun's low path across sky
she pauses   offers a strand of hair to
earth air fire water   asks for a sign from
the spirits of this place that
she may work with them

the next day by the leafless cherry
plum outside her window
the prayer tree on whose branches
she ties ribbons   the tree
to whom she offers sage, tea—
an imprint of owl's wings   circle of
feathers etched deeply in snow
sudden stop of mouse tracks
and at the base of the prayer
tree, a heart wind-carved in white

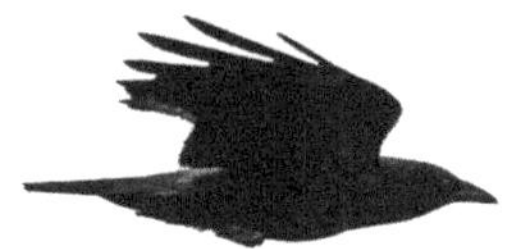

Alexandra Fidyk

Oh Silence
each of us begins
our life journey at your centre
our pilgrimage into otherness
circles out from you
some into sound
some not

Oh Silence
how scarce you have become
heavy snow in the poplars this morning
hoarfrost encasing branches and bales
magical beauty brings pause
remembrance
surrender

Oh Silence
a radiant orbit to truth
you ring all things, but where you dwell
creates weight, presence where motion
turns emptiness into meaning
births poetry and
beauty

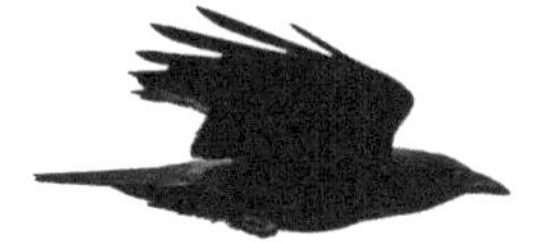

Lynn Fels

Across a Snowbound Field: A Snowy Leap into Metaphor

Mon pays ce n'est pas un pays, c'est hiver.
—Gilles Vignault, *Avec les vieux mots.*

Tracing presence across a snowbound field, your tracks leave me hungry for the touch of you. I chase your vanishing form, stumble, and shout your name, but you forge heedlessly forward. You insistently beckon and yet hinder my navigation in the snow. Flailing, knee-deep, I struggle to keep pace. Your strides and my stumbling disrupt the clear form of the field. "Wait for me," I yell. I scramble desperately to my feet; you plunge ahead; we race together on cross-country skis, pursued by yells and taunts of spectators. I hurl myself across an invisible barrier; my tumbled arrival recorded on the snow. "Looks like a snow angel crash-landed," the timekeeper jokes, as you, turning now towards me, pull me to my feet. You are laughing; your words undecipherable between the cheers; my heart in rhythmic turmoil; our exposed breath failed morse code in the frigid air. My body imprint remains testimony to my fall.

In snowshoes, you and I walk side by side, unspoken words between words spoken, small clouds in the cold air. A snow-blanketed field stretches across unknown lengths of time. Soon you will leave town to seek work in the city, and I, equally eager to flee the constraints of our lives, will fly to Vancouver to create a study of curiosity, a slow awakening, to what is present, here and now. We turn and see our snow tracks that give testimony to our struggles, as snowshoes break through thin sheets of snow crust, first a single track as we walked, one behind the other, then turning away to form individual lines of tracks, a metaphorical artifact of our journey. At times, our tracks unite, a pause, a consultation, a dialogue; at times, the distance between us reflects a wandering towards an encounter with a snowdrift, rabbit tracks, contemplation of what was, what is, what might be. How different our paths would have been, I say to you, if the snow had been able to bear our weight, or if only I alone was walking across this snowbound field. See there, where you pulled me up? A mélange of footsteps, as you tried to find your footing, and I reached up to receive your offered hand? How we walk and how the snow receives us documents our presence.

Cliff-jumping is a local sport known to only a few of us, those whose homes in our small town border on the golf course. Throughout winter, fresh fallen snow calls us to a cliff's edge, overlooking the river. Here, we choose pristine overhangs of snow, into which we dare each other, you go first, no you, then in tandem, run, leap, and slide down the cliff face, a falling in snow, an expanse of ice blue sky our horizon. Overhangs created by wind-swept snow are the best to leap into.

Imagine this. You are a snowflake, unique in your design, yet in the midst of a blizzard, your distinct presence is veiled. How might I imagine you in the midst of a crowd? How might we be present with each other? I open my mouth to catch falling snowflakes, and for the briefest moment, the cold touch of you awakens my tongue.

And yet…

You ride the chairlift up the side of the mountain, morning's sun lightens the horizon. Beneath your dangling skis, a ski trail, as yet unmarked, awaits. You will be the first to trace your presence. An artist, you see the unmarked snow as a blank canvas, desiring a painter's brush. Your skis, flexibility of body and shape of turns, announce your arrival; your choice of movement, direction, not yours alone to make. The canvas holds its own surprises.

But this telling moves too quickly, I want to linger with you in this snowbound field, to stay in a place that spells home to me, or race together hand in mittened hand across a finish line that spells a new beginning, or travel forward to that moment, après ski, hot cider, in the bar, giggling, our breath billowing in winter air as we tramp celebratory messages in the snow.

I recall the falling, legs buckling under me, snow sinking into openings of clothing, tops of boots, down my neck, your voice like a bite of wind, "come on, get up, you can do it," and I scramble to my feet, weighted by snow, and chase after you, determined to match your strides, your prints spaced just-out-of-reach so that after ten steps or maybe twelve, I can't remember now, I catch an edge, falling out of space, and collapse, crying "wait, wait for me" but you refuse to wait, your back receding, leaving an indecipherable track that those who follow stumble upon years later.

How do you read a tumbled bodyprint of scrambled motion and decipher the hunger for acceptance, approval, need to be in movement, to engage in the forbidden, to lose memory of all the hurts that sculpt each regrettable desire? You wouldn't have won, if I had refused, and winning then in those days was paramount, there was no alternative, this is what I had failed to recognize.

Riding the chair up into the morning's first rays, our coffee-run, we called it, you turn to me, "I love you." "Not now," I say, annoyed. "There's skiing to do." I have sabotaged your moment of confession. Evaded responsibility of declaration. I wait for your next move.

I am reminded of a game, each child armoured in snowsuit and winter boots, determined to vanquish the battlefield that was our childhood. "I'm king of the mountain!" someone shouts, bodies tumbling as first one, then another, seeks to topple the other from the peak of a snow-plowed mountains at the edge of our playground. Not once did we think to team up against the biggest kid, who wrestled, as if fighting for his life; singly we attacked, throwing ourselves against his legs, only to roll to the bottom, as one by one he dislodged us from his snowy throne. Yet still we persisted. To struggle again and again and again, arrested only by the sounding of the recess bell.

Beneath galaxies of stars, removing our snowshoes, we make snow angels "don't forget the halo!" imprinted snow holding the weight of our bodies, as we struggle to our feet laughing—"careful, don't step on the wing"— and throwing our arms around each other, hugging warmth into our bodies, together, we survey evidence of our presence, a flurry of angel-winged bodies populating the field in splendid disarray, a snowbound field where later, when this memory will have melted from view, remembered only now in this writing, they will come with dogs and sticks and beating back the tall grasses, find the body of a woman, an arm flung out as if reaching towards an unseen angel, come to rescue this child, this project, this idea from its ungodly moment.

Riding the chairlift at day's end, I note that your choreographed marks created on the canvas of snow are now criss-crossed with swoops and curves of fellow skiers, inspired by your initial artistry of that morning's blank canvas. Your marks are masked by the flurry of those who followed. No matter. What matters is your invitation, your offering.

You find your way to the cliff's edge, new fallen snow, and leap. You leap in hope. You leap in search of adventure. You leap out of your life. A noise cracks open a white expanse of snow, alerts you. High above the frozen crawl of river, the cliff releases its burden of snow with an unearthly groan. You twist to look, to identify what is happening, the consequence of your leap, as the weight of snow drops above you. A ragged wound tears itself along the cliff, revealing a fault line of earth and autumn grasses, just below the spot where you have only seconds earlier launched yourself into an overhang of fresh snow. Arms flailing, you ride the avalanche, swimming in snow, your only thought is to reach the river, scramble to safety beyond the train tracks, up and over, stumbling, finding your feet, tumbling down the embankment to the river where shards of ice floes crowd the shoreline. The tumultuous river of snow arrests in unsettling stillness around you. Shaken, you struggle to your feet to survey the broken terrain. Boulders, waist high, heavy chunks of broken snow obscure the train tracks that lead towards the town's paper mill. The enormity of your escape comes slowly to you.

To make a snow angel, find a white sheet of snow, and survey the canvas with care. There must be no clumsy leaps or floundering in the making of snow angels. A misplaced hand or careless imprint of snow boot is unforgivable; these lead to spoiled landscapes, marking the trespass of an ill-considered move. The first action is critical and must be performed with precision. Failure to execute is regrettable for there must be no repeated attempts, perfection is required, you may make only one snow angel. The first step is a bending of knees and swinging of arms to gather momentum, and then, a two-foot jump, with a 180-degree turn, so that you are standing backwards facing from where you have come, a gap between where you are now and where you once stood. Then comes freefall, with arms flung wide, a falling into an embrace of snow. Here is the difficult part, because if done hesitantly, or with caution, the impact of distributed weight will be corrupted, the snow canvas gouged by an errant elbow, or uneven leveling at the shoulders, or worse, evidence of an imposter's butt disturbing the sanctity of the art.

And now, lying on your back, your face exposed to open sky, pause to notice an unfamiliar weighting of body along a length of snow, the chilled presence of snow not yet seeping through snowpants, jacket, a snow-cloaked Earth that momentarily cradles you, without critique. This is as close to love that is possible for humans. Now, simultaneously sweep your arms and legs, open and closed, in the snow where you have fallen to claim a new space of presence; you are snow-painting in broad sweeps of motion. This is your moment of release—when embrace turns to signature. Now comes a final punctuation, for those of us who name ourselves as expert, the making of the halo, and in this you must be careful. This final gesture is what can ruin the snow painting, and so must be approached reverently yet boldly, to falter is draw one's hesitation into the snow. With a single mittened hand, arm raised directly behind and over your head, circle an oval in the snow. You must do this with the artistry of a calligrapher, the simplicity of a child artist. The snow angel is now complete. You are complete. Now a rescue helicopter arrives, its whirling blade sends snow skyward from snow-burdened boughs, a complicated maneuver, which allows you to be plucked from the ground, without disturbance to the snow angel, to be borne off to a distant city, while your brief presence remains marked in a snowbound field, witness only by resident winter birds. This would be the perfect escape, an unexplained disappearance for those following your trail. Yours would end here.

You and I ski the length of a moonlit trail, etch thin lines through snow, calligraphy of our presence. The pines are burdened with the weight of yesterday's snowfall, an owl calls, distant lights of the town flicker through the trees. Glide, glide, glide, motion of arms, legs, poles, skis in easy synchronization, our breath small cumulous clouds of condensation in the night air, a sprinkling of snowflakes like the aftermath of a snow globe shaken, as we watch entranced by the resettling of sparkles, my face wet, with melted snowflakes, tears, a swelling of joy, my heart moving in rhythm to your remembered breath upon my skin, your touch of fingers rising along the swell of my breast, how then shall I remember you, as you and I move through the darkness, your voice lost in the sound of wind in trees, we fall onto snowbound sheets, your arms cradling us, our bodies melt one into the other, a single pulse that carries us through the dark.

The skin of winter is peeling away. My slush-stained boots lie abandoned by the porch door. You pull back our kitchen curtains. The neighbourhood children, including ours, are building snow dams, mittened hands soaking wet, as they work together to reimagine their snowbound world. Streams of melting snow are corralled into strategically-placed dams, creating pools of water that stretch the width of the road. A car turns down our street, and then another. And then a third. Each driver hesitates before plunging their car into dammed unknown depths, releasing floods of water, leaving tire-treaded gouges in snow. Each time, after a car has passed by, the children refortify their dams, tramping snow like beavers with snow booted feet. A knock on the door. You are persuaded by a rosy-cheeked pair of bright-eyed twins, who have come to plead their case, shouting their approval as you say *yes, yes, yes* you will drive through their snow barriers. Just to see what happens. You struggle into your winter boots, shrug on your coat, and keys in hand, you get into your soon to be flooded minivan. Backing out of the driveway, you navigate through child-created flood plains, undoing what was created in anticipation of your arrival. You watch in your rear-view mirror, as children emerge from their secret hiding place—the neighbour's hedge—to repair the damage you have caused, and you keep driving, water rising, your foot pressed hard against the gas pedal, surrendering responsibility as they become pinpoints of undecipherable light creating new possible galaxies of imagination not ours.

References

Arendt, H. (1958). *The human condition.* University of Chicago Press.

Arendt, H. (1961). *Between past and future: Six exercises of political thought.* Viking.

Fels E., M. (2005). An exploration of the role of the skier as artist and mountain as canvas: The act of skiing, and the resulting tracks carved in the slope in relationship to Jackson Pollock's drip paintings, Earth Art and Performance Art. Unpublished essay. Emily Carr University. British Columbia.

Machado, A. (1930). Proverbios y cantqres (F. Varela Trans. 1987), (p. 63). In W. I. Thompson (Ed.), *GAIA, a way of knowing: Political implications of the new biology* (p. 4864). Lindisfarne.

Varela, F. (1987). Laying down a path in walking. In W. I. Thompson (Ed.), *GAIA, a way of knowing: Political implications of the new biology* (p. 4864). Lindisfarne.

Vignault, G. (1964), *Avec les vieux mots.* Editions de l'Arc.

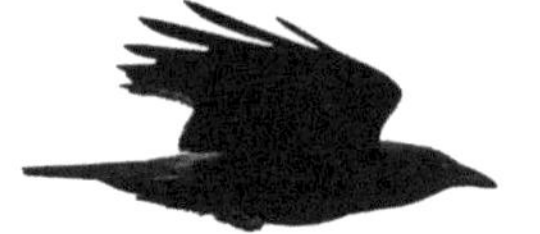

Jodi Latremouille

poetic grief-writing into the light

a movement towards resonance, towards kinship, towards generative dialogue,
towards our collective earth-healing—

slowly learning
our collective strength of spirit
the courage to be vulnerable,
to share the earthly mystery and profound beauty of love and loss, grief and praise—

an invocation to this communion

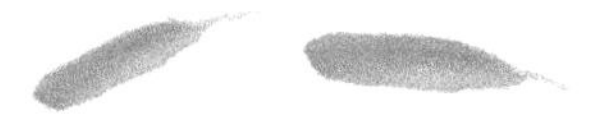

Latremouille, J. (2022). Found poem from Grief-writing. In A. Fidyk, & D. St. Georges (Eds.), Poetic Inquiry for synchrony & love: A new order of gravity [Special Issue]. *Art|Research International: A Transdisciplinary Journal*, *7*(2), 439-457.

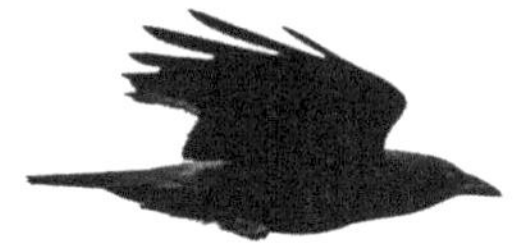

David W. Jardine

"The Associated Press Has Learned"

> We seek conversation not only in order to understand the other person better. We need it because our own concepts threaten to become rigid; the problem [can be] not that we do not understand the other person, but that we don't understand ourselves. We have the hermeneutical experience that we must break down resistance in ourselves if we wish to hear the other. (Gadamer, 2007, p. 371)

We must break down resistance in ourselves. I must break down resistance in myself. I must break down and seek the reassemble of the world if I wish to hear even my own words a soft distance away.

Our grandchild.
Just turned 7 months.
Been crawling a while.
Standing up and holding on.
And all those grandparent-y things that you talk too much about.
The soft curve of a pregnant belly. The new teeth.
The soft distance away. The parent's eye sparkles. The child's.
Too far to touch.
For now.
Safe.

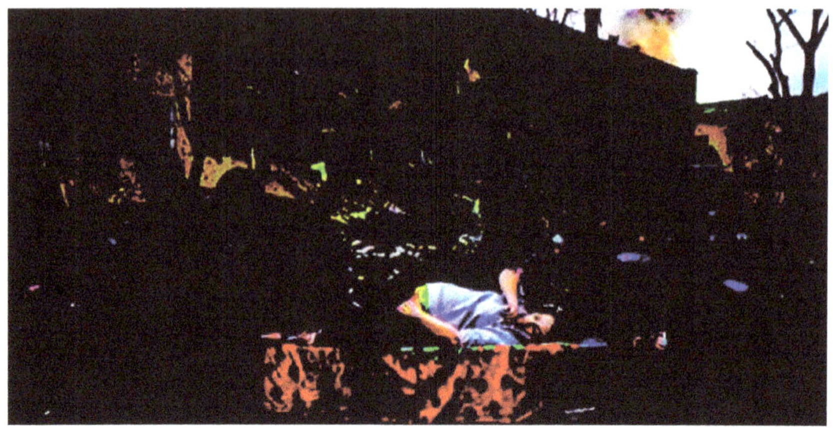

The Associated Press Staff (March 14, 2022). Pregnant woman, baby die after Russia bombing of maternity hospital. *CTVNEWS* Online: https://www.ctvnews.ca/world/pregnant-woman-baby-die-after-russia-bombing-of-maternity-hospital-1.5817994

"The Associated Press has learned"
"…she was meant to give birth"
"The Associated Press has learned"
"…an attack"
"The Associated Press has learned"
"…stroking her bloodied lower abdomen"
"The Associated Press has learned"
"…pelvis crushed and hip detached"
"The Associated Press has learned"
"'At least someone came to retrieve her,' they said"
"The Associated Press has learned"
"…so she didn't end up in the mass graves being dug for many"

Reference

Gadamer, H. G. (2007). Hermeneutics and the ontological difference. In R. Palmer (Trans. & Ed.), *The Gadamer reader: A bouquet of later writings* (pp. 356-371). Northwestern University Press.

Zena John

Chrysalis

Translucence contours your soul
Saturating your body with hopes, dreams, wishes
Stirring embers of faith in broad strokes
In your sacred moments a deep stillness gives way to
a roaring avalanche of pure power
jumpstarting your lacklustre emotional cocoon into overdrive
A new tomorrow beckons with your newfound resolve
Sense the new You, about to take flight

The Crown

Each life is so precious
Ego and the great divide disappear
We are but a poignant breath away from each other
Life dances through the breath we share
Some to sashay on Earth, others to fly beyond mortal borders
Reflect, reset and rekindle your childhood passions
The great equaliser is amongst us
No material wealth will spare anyone
The very breath we take for granted can be our last
Make the most of the time we have left
Reach out to loved ones
Do the thing that floats in your dreams
Give thanks for the life you have
Reach within and find the source of Divine Power
Everything… was inside of you all along

Axis

And so we turn away from the superfluous
We breathe in the daily rotation
O to see the Earth as a speck of cosmic dust
Is to fully appreciate our shared destiny

To visitors from behind the moon
We must be a curious lot
Fighting over crumbs
Blinded to the treasure threaded through our beings
The golden love-light knitting each to the other

Sanctum

Surging waterfalls of energy
Dance along my spine
Electrifying cells and space
The material vessel melts
The Void embraces me home
In this nothingness
All is revealed
My timeless form undulates in waves

Merle Nudelman

I Shall Know Why When Time is Over

after a line by Emily Dickinson

Through the hourglass
beat by beat
particles of being pass.

First the separations:
the squeeze and spark
slipping weeks

onto fine threads.
Metamorphosis:
reason's fantasy.

When next sensed
it perplexes—
this switch that hints

of the underside,

unsolvable riddles—
the curve of glass,

holograms flickering
on walls, the sweet
ring of atoms.

Time's questions
twist and turn,
Truth flickers.

Constant hourglass,
elliptical breath,
cryptic future past.

Spirit of Survival

My grandpa paces our hallways—
large hands clasped behind him,
        broad back straight,
        gaze infinitely kind.

I'll stay beside you, he promises.
All the way.
        In my dreams he grins,
        ready for the next joke—

Have you grown taller or am I
standing in a hole?
        Black hair slicked precisely,
        brown eyes crinkled at the corners

he beams bonhomie.
Standing to my left his ghostly hand
        squeezes my shoulder,
        suffuses my cells with certainty.

At 18 he lost parents and young sisters
suffocated in a lye-washed cattle car
        headed for Auschwitz.
        Torn, he'd stepped into the

work line with his older brother.
Together they watched their world
        go up in ashen bursts from
        the crematorium chimney.

In the munitions factory
he slaved for two,
        stole crusts of black bread,
        snaked along the dirt

under the guard's thick boot.
He survived the horror,
    tailored his way to Canada,
    rebuilt family while grieving.

My trials are small
and his blood pumps in my veins—
    ruddy with life, triumphant.
    Like grandpa I'm a survivor.

Primeval Piety

for Church at Yuquot Village (The Indian Church)
by Emily Carr

Bear witness:
    a white church kneels
in the wild heart of antiquity's forest,
its nuanced dark.

Grand leaves undulate,
    fan a hallowed presence.
Folding currents (a riotous blue-green)
form the soaring rib-vaults
    for nature's chapel
wherein these towering souls
recount the ages
    with sighs of lamentation.

Silos of light
    disperse then disappear.

Masked Regression

Misty with morning
she steps in to shower,
shuts sight
as water purifies
the slopes of her skin,
clearing blight.

She inhales the pause.
That scent.
Unearthly blooms,

perfumed souls
dust her palms
pressing skyward.

Towelled, creamed,
she tints cheeks, kohls eyes,
rouges lips prominent.

Feathery hair frames
her reflection benignly.
Fierce features tame.

The ancestral path recedes
when she slips into
skirt, sling-back shoes.

Vapours lift
and mask settles.
Ritual robes drape.

Around her the world
burns bright orange,
screaming.

Light in the Darkness of After

Five weeks in the ground, I visit mom in her sleep. I've heard
the keening, her soul's anguish, the plea: come before sunrise.
She longs to follow me. This can't be. Her work
is undone; little ones beckon.

In that dream, she visits a place where two children rest.
For me, there is no bed, no separate room. Only a recessed shelf
hollow as a box & facing the window. Mom frets.
Assure her I'm fine.

Deeply relaxed, she is permeated with glistening,
embraced by light that envelops her with infinite love.

At dawn that day her friend dreams. I entreat,
Tell mom I'm much better. They said I must eat & I'm eating.
Hands cupped before her, she approaches.

Another vision. Mom sees me laughing, biting into an apple.
Robust & sporting a red baseball cap, chatting with a friend. Later I don a suit.
Why? I was told to wear a suit. That I was going to judgement.
In an instant I'm transported elsewhere.

The Kabbalah teaches: a soul enters this world to fulfill a purpose.
Departing this earthly plane we waken in the spiritual realm. At the Heavenly Court
we learn where we failed and why.
The gavel falls . . .

Infinite Reverie

Do you remember how you came into existence?
You may not remember / because you arrived a little drunk.
Let me give you a hint:
Let go of your mind & then be mindful./ Close your ears & listen!
from *Ripened Fruit*, Rumi

Floating from bed to courtyard
in early morning haze
fleeting you find me by your side.

While I recline in another sphere
you enter the hall & sit at the table
then watch me cough, dab eyes with cloth
proffered by my hooded guide.

Despite your plea I take my leave
and ask as reassurance,
Do you remember how you came into existence?

Forty days since my death—
thirty-six festive candles flickered, waned.
Your essence sinks, soul wails inside cells.
The healer's hands pause.
When your eyes detect the brilliance,
dubious mind rethinks, clears.

Soon you are gold, enfolded in presence,
the love I send into the shards—
to birth, to the angel's stroke above your lips.
You may not remember because you arrived a little drunk.

I make clouds, rain, even sun's rays
while you rest, invoke my name.
Empty hands fill with familial light.

Wisps, vistas: walls with raised roses
& dahlias, perfumed silver snow,
the flit-fade of endless faces.

Blink and you are soaring
above the ageless gorge
where rivers murmur, glint.
Let me give you a hint.

On the dock you become air—
distorting waves, lifting mallards.
Suffused with luminosity you are
breath, moons, the constant
drift of rushing sky & water.

Patterned bark,
even islands on the horizon
merge into infinity.
Let go of your mind, then be mindful.
Close your ears & listen.

Skewed Perceptions

The mirrored visage flows
beneath thick thumbs
moulding molecules,
disparate parts:

the Cubist angles of identity.
She retreats from
the female returning her gaze—
the lie of her eyes, temple hills,

malleable mouth.
Hands scan
shadow-valleys,
flinch

with the surprise of
separateness.
She tasks her fingers,
lightly probes

this other self—
cast, animated,
her avatar—
a brilliant tile vibrating

a looped mosaic.
Three exhalations.
She reaches for the mist—
mist that she is—

claims flesh and sinew,
resumes the count:
the dips and kicks
of a textured tango.

Megan Davis

poetic imagination
connective tissue for dialogue and creative leaps

—across nations, hemispheres, and epochs—

neither securely anchored in locality
nor free-floating and rootless in globality

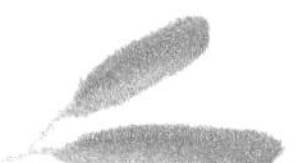

Davis, M. (2022). Found poem from Exiled poetics: Glück, Darwish, and a transnational edenic imagination. In A. Fidyk, & D. St. Georges (Eds.), Poetic Inquiry for synchrony & love: A new order of gravity [Special Issue]. *Art|Research International: A Transdisciplinary Journal, 7*(2), 351-368.

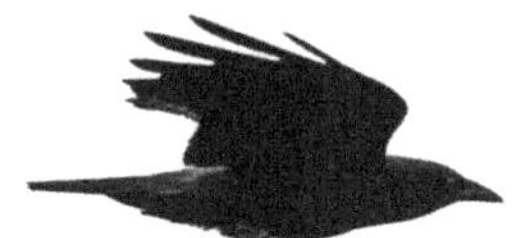

Melaina Weiss, Karen Weiss, James Harley, & Brandon MacLeod

Teaching as Felt and Poetic

The poet as teacher, human as poet, teacher as human. They all feel the same to me. (Lorde, 2020, p. 182)

Whoever writes in blood and aphorisms does not want to be read but to be learned by heart. (Nietzsche, 1995, p. 40)

Teaching-Feelings Within Animate Poetics. What does it feel like to teach? How do we emphasize the *feel* of the experience of teaching without distilling the exploration down to concepts and codes to be analyzed? How do we renew poetics as a way of being, without turning it into something methodical? How do we keep explorations of feeling in a space that accepts feeling as both knowable and unknowable? Our exploration of feeling and its character stems from Nietzschean ideas of embodiment. For Nietzsche, the "body, perception and language are all intertwined" and are situated in the world that is "a dynamic and changing field" (Torjussen, 2009, p. 180). In Nietzsche's view, it is impossible to grasp lived experience and so all language is metaphor (Torjussen, 2009). Metaphor and the perceiving, situated living body all point to an embodiment of sorts, and that embodiment is central to what is meant by feeling—the sense of the entanglement of body, language, world, and perception. Nietzsche's embodiment cannot encapsulate the totality of feeling. We add another dimension of feeling that is spirit or energy associated with the cosmos and the experience of the other within ourselves.[10] Entanglement of body and language

[10]. Here I have adopted and adapted the phrase "the Other inside us" from Darlene St. Georges (2019, p. 717). St. Georges explores the question of what it is "to experience the Other within us?" (p. 720) in a creation-research paradigm that embraces the techniques of the poetic. Nietzsche's concept of embodiment is too personal and not integrated enough to allow St. Georges' important question its due. Adding the conception of "the Other inside us" engages the total lived experience of feeling both individually and together with the other in educative moments.

points to language and poetics as a confluence; Abram (2017) links language to the sensuous world where "language as a bodily phenomenon accrues to *all* expressive bodies, not just the human (p. 80). Including the individual in conceptions of feeling is necessary, but confining feeling to the individual precludes what we can know in relation to feeling; "welcoming other epistemologies, ontologies and cosmologies that reflect an organic inclusive and emergent world, where knowledge is not confined to the individual, challenges what it is to know and what is of value" (Fidyk, 2013, p. 398). Nietzsche's embodiment is centered around the individual, and though feeling has to do with the individual, it does not always come from the individual nor is it always centered around the individual. Feeling is a movement of chest embedded in an expanse of rolling hills, peppered with scrubby brush and river running through it. Feeling is losing a sense of self in Kathleen Munn's painting Horses (1927). Feeling is a movement of my interdependent body with my daughter's as we dance together in a moment of song. Feeling is dynamic lived paradox.

Explorations of feeling here flow forth in paradoxical, dynamic, and animate paradigms, that allow feeling between all possible relations of the individual, the other, land, place, and the cosmos. Our poetic explorations, alongside feelings-in-teaching or our teaching-feelings, are situated in an animated paradigm (Fidyk, 2013; 2016). Fidyk (2016) expresses the webscape of an animated paradigm:

> An animated world is organic, paradoxical, in flux, dynamic, fluid, intentional and inclusive of its own values. Reality here acknowledges the role of the unconscious as inherently creative and in part unknowable yet always alive and present. It honours the sacredness, the livingness and soul of the cosmos. To situate oneself in a worldview that includes and values the unconscious, transpersonal, transgenerational, transspecies, feeling (function), imaginal and emergent dimensions is to radically reconsider the ways that we come to know and thereby what we know. (p. 56)

As feeling is paradoxical and arises both individually and inter/intra/trans-relationally, exploring a question of feeling-in-teaching (where there are always multiple others) would be seriously limited in a paradigm that does not respect or recognize the integral relational complexity of emergences of feeling. We choose an animated paradigm because all of us as poets and authors exist in one; also, not only does it allow paradoxicality, it encourages paradoxicality. The paradigm breathes; it makes space for a breadth of possibility in exploring teaching-feelings.

Poetic exploration of teaching-feelings. The process for exploring feelings-in-teaching and teaching feelings arose from discussions with another teacher. We were talking about how it feels to teach; what feelings arise within, without, from, alongside, etc., educative moments in teaching. The idea of a poetic exploration of teaching-feelings emerged from that discussion. That we both exist in poetic ways of being predates the conversation that spurred us forward. What would it be to have teachers write poems in relation to moments of teaching? Embracing poetics was intentional and spontaneous, as Bhattacharya (2020) points out, it can be a process where "the practice itself becomes the site of inquiry" (p. 166). We consider our exploration in line with Fidyk's and St. Georges' (2022) characterization of Poetic Inquiry as a way of being; "poetic inquiring extends from the arrival of a question or through the midst of a problem into wondering, noticing, imaging, and breaks forth in one or more intentional and/or spontaneous forms of expression" (p. xi).

For this exploration, the term teacher is used in a very broad sense—the only requirement for someone to qualify as having taught, was that they[11] could imagine a time when they had taught someone else—and identified the experience with 'what it feels like to teach.' Such a broad conception of teaching is to refrain from limiting "teaching" to dominant conceptions of teaching. Some of our greatest teachers have had no institutional affiliation. Some of our greatest teachers are not even human.

Poetic Suite. The first poem was offered after the aforementioned discussion. The second three poems (for a total of four poems in the suite) were written in response to considering an event of teaching and that event's associated feelings. Contributors were encouraged to write what they were called to write. The following are the animated poetic explorations of feeling-in-teaching and teaching-feelings, engaged in by four contributors. Each of the four contributors wrote one poem in the spirit of Poetic Inquiry. All four contributors are creative co-authors of this work, responding to the question *what does it feel like to teach?*

[11]. We use they as both singular and plural pronouns to promote gender inclusive language here and elsewhere in the paper.

Untitled

I threw at you a barrage of words.
adjectives verbs nouns what I
thought of as descriptive and
interesting and thought provoking
and you looked at me with those
wide blue eyes and nodded.
I wondered but I knew

I handed you a piece of clay and
said. Close your eyes and make me
something. You did as you were
told. A bird emerged and flew away

Next a twirl of the kaleidoscope
causing colours falling all around
making a brand new pattern to
wonder at

And then you say something that is
so full of truth that I laugh and
repeat your wisdom to anyone who
will listen

Some days you and I just need to do
the tried and true and that works

You keep me on my toes dreaming
of ways to reach you with the
wisdom of the ages. And some days
you reach out to me with the
wisdom of the ages

We will keep trying you and I, we
are gifted with each other for this
reason.

Words and colours and the feel of
clay. I want to reach you, not with the
promise of gifts but with the gift of
promise, and you freely thinking for
yourself and flying away

Mountain Sense

Considering life and mellow climbs forming cosmic bonds beyond recognition, beyond indictment. Leaving matte moments to fade
forever while contours last lifetimes. It's like god should be more chill.
It's like god should be more wild.

Late start, catching 36 degrees and midday sun. Rushing,
unconsidering too much, up and around corners until the Cariboo-Mountain casual grip on reality loosens and Buddha descends to the sediment below, lost among the great mystery.

Forging ahead, the end point: a lake and cabin at the peak, east of the Rocky Mountain Trench; across Highway 16, over the Fraser River; through Dunster, parallel to Pete's road; past thick forests to stick forests and streams; just the end point on my mind. Only my body and a mountain in between.

Bleak and blurry and alone, barely able to escape, trees thinning, rocks stuck out their claws. Heat stroke and a plague of mosquitoes do wonders to wobble wonderment and beg trembling steps.

Gather it together, among shade and outside tea. Mind, body, and soul in particular - shirtless, sweating excessively, and slightly blood stained. The turn-around-to-survive move. Slow ride and contemplation-made. Corners come smooth, like god got me chill. The shine of something breaks twilight.

Buddha's eternally awaiting. Here I am, still wandering and wondering. Still alive. Safe return back to the garlic bulbs from where we came.

Spaghetti and sauce simmering through screened windows, red wine spilling out the speakers of life, an arrival of any kind is worth celebrating. We cheers, and the two old men call it "Mountain Sense," tell me about life, lifetimes and their home.

Every Single Time

Fuck
Any minute now.
How do I look?
Oh well. Too late.
They can see right through me.
Fraud!
No, Focus.
You're here for them.
Leadership.
Citizenship.
Pedagogy.
Hope my foot hasn't reached my mouth.
Body Liberation.
Anthropocene.
Clapping. Finally.
Questions?
Whew, I'm glad you learned something.

On Different Days

the pose.
on different days.
each muscle turn twist stretch and ache
each movement of living in place
on different days.

an outstretched toe
pointed out the length of my leg
loose and taut hovering
the instant before it strikes the ground
to spring with and from the dirt packed trail.

a lunge and bent knee
to push forward my moving groin
strained from past injury
inside leg-to boot-to ski-to snow
-to move just right
from the changing slide on snow and ice.

even when it's always the same
different days different ways different place
and. then. slide. muscles to contract and extend into
a relaxed alert peaceful warrior
ready in still movement

slide into moving movement
share a shovel. share a pick. share an axe
share a pose
become the tool
move to fit. this time. in a groove

but never just so
or
ever like so

the

next

time.

Expressing Teaching-Feelings in *a world that speaks.*[12] To analyze these poems would be to take them out of an animated paradigm. To comment on our specific feelings, connections, relations and engagements would be to take those unfettered possibilities away from other readers.[13] To conclude, this section is a mere reflecting on some elements of feeling-in-teaching as situated in an animated paradigm in relation to the suite of poems. The animate poetic explorations allow for paradox, breadth and depth of feeling, inner/outer relations and a place to research that could never be results driven. Exploring feeling through poetry is both knowable and unknowable. In each reading, taking time with each poem, offers a vast and varied sensorium of feeling—some with a sense of mineness, and much more coming from elsewhere and other. Each poem is so distinct, offering different subjectivities tied to different places, spaces, identities, relations, and inner and outer experience. Associating the poems together, there exists a synthetic impression of our teachers and our students and the non-human others included in what teachers and students might be. St. Georges (2019) identifies the power of reading (and performance of) poetry as something that can center simultaneously inner/outer relationality and how these partake with each other in an integral way. "Poems can create spaces for

12. David Abram (2017) uses the phrase "a world that *speaks*" (p. 81), to emphasize that language is part of an animate and integral web. He elucidates "Our own speaking, then, does not set us outside of the aminate landscape but—whether or not we are aware of it—inscribes us more fully in its chattering, whispering, soundful depths" (p. 81). We think that this kind of view of language and fleshy and interdependent and related and expressive bares the kind of Poetic Inquiry that is a way of being (Fidyk & St. George, 2022), rather than confined to method. We use this phrase here to evoke the depth and interrelatedness in each poetic expression of feeling-in-teaching and teaching feelings.

13. We did write our own personal reflections on our own poems, but chose not to use those reflections. After we discussed the poems and listened to the reader's engagements, we thought the writer's reflective position should be omitted and not included in how we expressed and presented the poems. The personal reflections illuminated the individual author. We thought that our own personal reflections would influence how a reader would engage with the feelings-in-teaching and teaching-feelings that were being expressed poetically. While such an influence is never a good or bad thing, we all agreed that if we omitted those reflections, the relations, land, place, others, and cosmic players in each poem could take up more space and be allowed more of their own expression.

love to enter into our NOW and facilitate our coming to know ourselves and others relationally—a place/space where we can submerge and emerge in a dialogue of our shared humanity" (2019, p. 711). To read these poems individually and in relation is a sort of working on the poetry in an intimate manner. When we *work* on the poems, the poems work on us; Bhattacharya (2020), describes a similar iteration of Poetic Inquiry. There is a connective sense of our taste of either the author's feeling or the cosmic feeling of teaching, because the feeling emerging in each reading of these poems, are not ones that could be said to simply have a sense of mine; the human, non-human and cosmic others are present. The kaleidoscopic offering in *Untitled*, the affects of mosquitoes on a tired body in *Mountain Sense*, the gaze of the other in *Every Single Time*, and the movement seeking out a good fit in *On Different Days,* all emphasize feelings-in-teaching and teaching-feelings as co-emergent, co-existing and co-created. We include an individual, but the knowledge of feeling is not contained or constrained by the individual.

Living and being poetically expresses *something else* within our teaching-feelings; certainly, poetic framing is one possible way of touching the knowable, but also grazing the unknowable, as *it* raises the hairs, shrinks the shoulders, tightens the skin, or opens the chest. We peek into the others that affect us. In this suite of poems there is an authentic and enlivening exploration of the question—What does it feel like to teach?—though not a clearly expressible one. If the reader manifests the dynamic and animate, even though each poem has an *I*, the *I* can remain paradoxically included, centered, and *decentered* so that we can abandon "a privileging of individual knowing" and promote "ways of knowing through the collective and personal unconscious, the realm of the ancestors and through intimate relation with the natural world" (Fidyk, 2013, p. 385). In a true sense of animated, we can momentarily become each teaching subjectivity (though never in their entirety) and get a sense of the inter/intra/trans-relational that inheres in teaching-feeling subjectivities. Poetry, poetics, and poets can tell us at the very least *something else* about the relations that inhere in feeling; Nietzsche's (1996) sense of how feeling communes with its surroundings is expressed in his following sentiment about the poets:

> This, however, all poets believe: that whoever pricks up his ears as he lies in the grass or on lonely slopes will find out *something* about those things that are between heaven and earth. And when they feel tender sentiments stirring, the poets always fancy that nature herself is in love with them; and that she is creeping into their ears to tell them secrets and amorous flatteries; and this they brag and boast before all mortals (emphasis added). (p. 128)

He points to the experience of being aroused by different instances of the Other. He is glib, but honoured and proud to hear *others.* Unlike Nietzsche, in our poetic explorations, the individual (hearing-tasting-sensing-touching-feeling human and non-human others) is never assumed to be the biggest and most profound player. Yet, to commune in the paradox of feeling, we too, *with humility* brag and boast and are honoured in our feeling emerging with/from cosmic, social, human and non-human others. Finally, we are humbled and grateful to express it through animate and dynamic poetics.

References

Abram, D. (2017). *The spell of the sensuous. Perception and language in a more than human world.* Vintage Books.

Bhattacharya, K. (2020). Cultivating resonant images through poetic meditation: A de/colonial approach to educational research. In E. Fitzpatrick, & K. Fitzpatrick (Eds.), *Poetry, method and education research doing critical, decolonising and political inquiry* (pp. 155-171). Routledge.

Fidyk, A. (2013). Conducting research in an animated world: A case for suffering. *International Journal of Multiple Research Approaches,* *7*(3), 384-400.

Fidyk, A. (2016). Locating research in and animated world: reconceptualising design. *Esoterismo Ocidental: Estudos Jungianos-O Homem Moderno em Busca da Alma, 2,* 47-61. https://recil.grupolusofona.pt/bitstream/10437/7624/3/Ata%20Estudos%20 Junguianos%20V2.pdf

Fidyk, A., & St. Georges, D. (Eds.). (2022). Editorial Poetic Inquiry for synchrony & love: A new order of gravity. *Art/Research International: A Transdisciplinary Journal,* *7*(2), x-xiv.

Fitzpatrick (Eds.), *Poetry, method and education research doing critical, decolonising and political inquiry* (pp. 51-60). Routledge.

Fitzpatrick, K. (2021). Writing the university through poetry: The pleasure of scholarship against the spike of neoliberalism. In E. Fitzpatrick & K. Fitzpatrick (Eds.), *Poetry, method and education research: Doing critical, decolonising and political inquiry* (pp. 97-103). Routledge.

Lorde, A. (2009). *I am your sister: Collected and unpublished writings of Audre Lorde.* Oxford University Press.

Nietzsche, F. (1996). *Thus spoke Zarathustra: A book for all and none.* The Modern Library.

Prendergast, M. (2021). Education and/as art: A found poetry suite. In E. Fitzpatrick & K. Fitzpatrick (Eds.), *Poetry, method and education research doing critical, decolonising and political inquiry* (pp. 51-60). Routledge.

St. Georges, D. (2019). Relational poetic encounters: Opening spaces at Tate Liverpool. *The International Journal of Art & Design, 38*(3), 710-722.

Torjussen, L. P. S. (2009). Is Nietzsche a phenomenologist: Towards a Nietzschean phenomenology of the body. In A-T. Tymieniecka (Ed.), *Analecta Husserliana CIII* (pp. 179-189). Springer Science.

Sarah MacKenzie-Dawson

Marrow wakes
deep hearted breath
that stirs the spirits

We love

becoming present—
in tune with breath and one another,
in tune with Earth-Creation

a way of being
of spirit, of truth, of liminality, of reflection—

a sacred truth.

MacKenzie-Dawson, S. (2022). Found poem from Breathing within the echoes of circular (uncertainty). In A. Fidyk, & D. St. Georges (Eds.), Poetic Inquiry for synchrony & love: A new order of gravity [Special Issue]. *Art|Research International: A Transdisciplinary Journal*, *7*(2), 415-438.

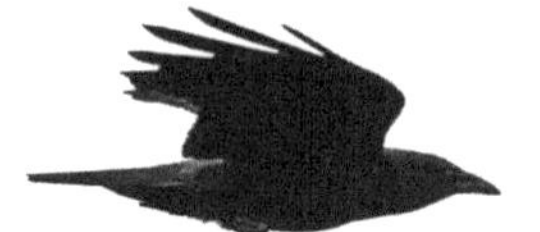

Laura Apol

Inheritance: Paradoxes of Love, Learning, and Loss

In my academic life, I have had many opportunities to work in global contexts and to travel internationally for research and for study. One such opportunity took me to Indonesia, where we, as a group of Michigan State University faculty and students, considered issues of equity and diversity (among them cultural, ethnic, geographic, linguistic, and religious) as they played out in local and national educational contexts. I had a central role in planning the study program, but it was not until I arrived in Jakarta that I fully realized the ways my own personal, ethnic, and familial history intersected with the Indonesian lives and histories around me. Born in the United States, I am Dutch by heritage, the granddaughter and great-granddaughter of settlers who came to the Midwest from the Netherlands in the late 1800s and early 1900s. Being Dutch by heritage means I am also part of the colonial history of the islands of Indonesia, once referred to as the Dutch East Indies. More directly, my paternal great-grandfather lived for a time in Indonesia before returning to Holland and then emigrating to the United States.

At the start of my first visit, the connections I made between the Netherlands and Indonesia were, to me, intriguing and sometimes charming. I had grown up in a community that was proud and protective of its Dutch roots, and in Jakarta I recognized words (straat, vlinder), icons (the windmill cut-out towering over the bakery), and foods (koeken, Rijsttafel) that reflected my Dutch heritage. But, as I learned more, I realized that behind these moments of overlap was the reality that my history is the history of colonization. The Dutch were cruel conquerors, hard taskmasters who grew rich at the expense of the culture and heritage of the islands of Indonesia.

What began as a study tour soon led to collaborations with Indonesian scholars, and I made a half-dozen trips to Indonesia before the pandemic interrupted those possibilities. Each trip was filled with learning, but it was the poetry I wrote during the first trips that most clearly represent my personal and cultural discoveries. Those early poems find points of connection and points of departure; they interrogate my family history, they question the ways Indonesian educators and students viewed our visits, and they reveal my growing appreciation of the Indonesian acceptance of diverse religious perspectives—so different from my homogenous Dutch Calvinist upbringing. As well, they acknowledge my own positioning as a beneficiary of colonialism—an academic exploring equity and diversity in a country that harbours my own ghosts, and an American of Dutch heritage recognizing the exquisite beauty of the islands around me.

These, then, are the poems that tell the story of my early visits to Indonesia—a story of cultural and familial inheritance and of the paradoxes of love, learning, and loss.

Lesson 1: The paradox of faith

I began writing at dawn on the first morning when I heard, for the first time, the call to prayer that roused the city in the dark. The call came from all-around, a clamour of amplified voices that rose and fell in different tonal sameness. I found it beautiful and stirring—strange and deeply sacred.

First Morning in Jakarta

It is the call to prayer, *azan*, that wakes
me, a summons that stretches
across the city, rises
to my room
on the seventeenth floor

—is joined by another, and another,
a cacophony of lifting, of falling,
a reminder
of what it means to be faithful,

and I stand at the window
to get my bearings in this city
so far from home.

Which direction is holy,

and what, today, could convince me
to kneel?

*

Thick haze obscures
the stars, but constellations
scatter below—streetlights,
headlights, a kitchen here,
a bedroom there,
the yellow glow
of a porch bulb left on against the dark.

High-rise offices,
sleek metal and glass by day,
are silent sarsens
before the rising sun.

* This is morning in Jakarta,
night's angels
ascending as *fajr* gives way
to city sounds: a motorcycle's whine,
the tap of a taxi's horn.

In the distance,
the train rumbles through,
one long ribbon of sound, each
florescent car over-bright and filled,

ferrying the waking world
across the city, transport from one life
to the next.

Lesson 2: The paradox of memory

The first evening in Jakarta, we were treated to a coffee (*kopi*) demonstration, complete with authentic Dutch *stroop koekjes* (syrup-waffle cookies). I was delighted by the event; both the coffee and the cookies were a recognizable cultural connection to my childhood and brought back to me the smells and sounds of my grandmother's kitchen. My writing about that memory is filled with familial love. What the poem leaves unsaid is that coffee in Indonesia is a direct result of colonization; plants were brought to Java during the Dutch occupation in order for the Netherlands to break into the worldwide coffee trade, and European fortunes were made from island resources and labour. In the poem, there is no irony (or maybe, unconsciously, there is) in the notion that for a Dutch-heritage woman, the coffee and cookie are, both personally and historically, *for you.*

Crossed Culture

The day ends with a coffee tasting:
Old Java notes of citrus and floral, tobacco,
chocolate and smoke.

So many ways
to make a perfect cup—
filter cone, French press, vacuum pot.
And here is what is needed: fresh-roasted beans,
burr mill grinder, filtered water, a thermometer
and scale.

Grind coarsely…
Measure carefully…
Heat gradually…
Pour slowly…

Bloom the coffee the demonstrator instructs,
stirring
with a small wooden paddle,

and I think
of the first coffee I knew that blossomed,
the aroma filling my grandmother's house.

A battered percolator
with a glass bubble in the lid;
mountain-grown Folgers
in a red can that exhaled
when she pressed the opener through its tin lip;
water from the tap, an eggshell in the basket—
the gas flame turned up high.

Her coffee was never science;
it was music. It was art. At first, a silence;
then the rattle of innards, and the burp of liquid
in the percolator's small glass globe,

darkening from water-clear to chestnut-brown—
burbling faster, the rich smell
steaming
the windows. She'd sit with me then—
pour us each a pink Melmac cup,
offer a windmill cookie
to dip and slurp.

Tonight, they serve the *kopi* sample
in a tasting carafe
along with single-packaged *stroop koekjes.*
Each plastic wrapper is printed with a tag
that reads, in Dutch, *for you.*

Lesson 3: The paradox of history

In the heart of Jakarta is Batavia Square—the capital and trading center of the Dutch East Indies, located in the heart of Old Town. The Square is surrounded by buildings of Dutch architecture: City Hall, the Post Office; several colonial-era banks, residences, and warehouses now serving as museums and galleries.

Under one of the buildings, we were shown a prison from colonial times, and I suddenly wondered about the man who was my great-grandfather. As a young Dutch man in Indonesia, it is likely that he was either a criminal transported to and serving a sentence in Indonesia, or a soldier stationed there. Might this prison—or one like it—have been part of his story? And if it was, what options, if any, might his story contain? Did I hope he had been a criminal or a soldier, one without rights or one with power? Did I want him to have suffered or to have caused suffering? And what, then, was my birth-right, my inheritance when faced with the prison door?

Colonial History

There are stories that are forever
untold. My grandfather's father—

how do I know this?
Before I set foot in the islands,
before I could find them on a map,
I inherited the word: *Indonesia.*

Was he a soldier? Was he a prisoner?
He was never a wealthy man,
so what are the other options
for this tale?

I cannot avoid the threshold
to the prison under the city hall,
where he crosses into this story—

one side of the metal door
or the other.

They made the ceiling so low
a person could not stand up.

They let the floods come in—
let the rooms fill with terror and tides.

What, then, do I wish for the ending:
that he found himself in rising water

or that he was the one
                    who'd locked the door?
                                        (Apol, 2018, p. 20)

Lesson 4: The paradox of prayer

While Islam is the dominant religion in Indonesia, there are a number of official religious traditions that are represented and recognized by the government. Christian churches and Catholic cathedrals exist beside mosques, and just outside Jakarta are two large and historic UNESCO sites—one Buddhist, one Hindu. The next two poems convey the ways these various religious traditions, set side-by-side, invited me to explore my own spiritual understandings. The following poem takes place at Borobudur, the world's largest Buddhist temple, located in Central Java. The Pièta can be found in Jakarta's Church of Our Lady of Assumption; directly across the street from the Cathedral stands the Istiqlal (Independence) Mosque, the largest mosque in Southeast Asia. My prayers and requests for blessing drew from each of these traditions.

Surrender

> Attachment is the root of suffering
> —Gautama Buddha

You walk up Borobudur in silence,
circling each level of the temple sun-wise
three times. It is a lesson

in cut stone, in carvings,
in bell-shaped *stupas* that point the way
to heaven, each step a practice

in loosening desire.
The guide says on the seventh level
you can make your personal request

for blessing. You circle and climb. Circle
and climb. With each footfall,
you hold your daughter

in your mind. Yesterday, at the Pièta,
you lit a candle; tomorrow,
you will cover your head,

bare your feet in the mosque.
You are desperate
for an ear that is listening.

Like the saffron-robed monks who bow
with each breath, with each step
you hold
          and let go.

(Apol, 2018, p. 45)

Lesson 5: The paradox of blessing

Like "Surrender," the following poem again draws from the multiplicity of religious traditions recognized in Indonesia. Having been raised in a homogeneous and monotheistic environment, I loved the ways these many faith traditions coexisted in close proximity. In addition to Borobudur and the Christian churches of Old Jakarta, "Here, the Holy" brings in three additional religious sites: Prambanan, an 8th-century Hindu temple compound outside Yogyakarta, dedicated to the Trimūrti, the expression of God as the Creator, the Preserver, and the Destroyer; Mount Merapi, a volcano with spiritual significance in the creation stories of the Javanese; and a *pesantran*, which is a Muslim boarding school.

Here, The Holy

At the square of Jakarta,
in the crucifix glare
of white marble history,
I pick up a stone.

To the chanting of monks
ascending the stairs of Borobudur,
I pick up a stone.

I pick up a stone
as the sun sets
on the temple spires of Prambenan,
and as the sun rises
on the spirits that re-green Merapi's burn.
At the *pesantran*,
while the young girls watch
from their crowded rooms,
I pick up a stone.

Such heft of history

—the cross of a steeple,
the monks' meditation,
the looking-on children;

such solid holiness,
here in my hand.

Lesson 6: The paradox of the ancestors

My time in Indonesia made me feel closer to many aspects of my own history and ancestry. This was especially true in Bali, where home temples to the ancestors stood in each family compound and offerings of flowers and rice were placed in doorways, on street corners, under trees, on dashboards of cars, and in restaurants, shops, offices, and schools. I was aware that around me were echoes of my own past—not only my cultural and colonial heritage, but my personal ancestry as well.

Crossroad

The Balinese know
a crossroad is a sacred space.

I stood for a long time,
waiting for the ancestors
to speak. They forgot
they were my guides,

or the words they said
were lost
to the morning roosters
and the pounding waves.

Each caged bird
has its own song, a voiceprint
from a wooden perch.
Each flower turns toward light.
I have returned to this crossroad
alone. I am here
to make an offering to the gods.

Lesson 7: The paradox of power

Part of my time in Indonesia was intended to be a chance to learn directly about enactments of formal education, on both a national and a local level. Our group visited primary and secondary schools, universities, boarding schools, religious institutions, and private academies funded by wealthy donors and corporations. To demonstrate the nuances of their programs, many of these groups took us on campus tours, some of which included observing students in classrooms. At one institution, the guide took great pride in telling us how well the students, who had been brought from a local island to live and study at the school, performed on the national math exams. The guide told us that these students—having had little access to book learning before arriving at the school—now learned with astonishing speed and accuracy; as we watched, he shouted out math problems to be solved by the students (some of whom were very young) at a white board in the front of the room. Later, these same students donned their traditional clothing and *performed* for us once again—this time a cultural dance that included instruments and drums from their island home.

Throughout the school, on each glass door and window there were signs that read, both in English and in Indonesian, "This is glass"—intended to keep students from bumping into or, worse, breaking through the panes. To me, the signs seemed indicative of all I was observing: that these students, repeatedly asked to perform for strangers, were enclosed by glass walls that were unfamiliar and that kept them apart from their homes, their families, and each other. It was highly competitive to attend this school, and it assured these students a life away from the island where they had been born. But I wondered if, after all, they considered this an opportunity when set against the costs they seemed to incur.

Student Performance

This is glass —this the clear pane,

the schoolyard scorch of sun beyond, blurred
in the haze of Jakarta's mid-afternoon.

Here are the Maluku students
—spice island songs and iridescent beads—
performing for guests—geometry and fractions,
traditional dance
. . . look what they can do.

Here is the price the promise
of a better life. Mica memories of home:

seas of glass and seaglass,
silica sand and fire

left behind,   hunger driving
each dream,

replaced now by the unseen door,

the invisible wall.   For the chosen,
beware—   *This is glass.*

Lesson 8: The paradox of grace

Sometimes when we visited schools, young children wanted to touch my skin. Often, they asked for a photo and stepped alongside if a camera appeared. Through these experiences, I felt the weight of my intrusion as an observer—a white woman from a U.S. institution of higher education. As well, I felt the weight of my history as a person of Dutch descent and discomfort at the thought of a great-grandfather who had lived and walked on these islands, in a capacity I did not know. One day, on a bicycle ride down a mountain, I saw a butterfly on the path ahead. Before I could swerve or stop, I had overtaken it and my tire had run across it. But as I continued, it preceded me again on the path, and I realized I had only run over the shadow; the butterfly itself was above me, ahead, and flying on. The experience brought to mind questions about inherited responsibility and release. The answer, I concluded, was not either/or; it was both/and. Yes, responsibility. Yes, release.

Yes, grace in the everyday.

Grace

On the bicycle path ahead, a butterfly,
perfect wings, erratic flight.
Before I can stop, it is caught
under my wheels

—but it is only its shadow
that is crushed—

the shadow-shape
still fluttering further along the path,
the blue wings overhead
still moving through light.

Why, then, this grief?

In the village, dogs eat the rice
from the offerings in the doorways.
In the village, chickens eat the rice
from the offerings in the doorways.

Maybe the spirits are angry.

Or maybe this is the nature of grace:
to see the shadow and notice the wings;
to taste the grain, offered in prayer—
for a moment, to be one
with the gods.

Lesson 9: The paradox of beauty

Throughout my time in Indonesia, I learned not only history and culture, not only religion and education, not only the weight of colonialism and the on-going pressures of western influence. I learned, as well, the exquisite loveliness of the islands. I found solace in the skies and ocean, in the mountains and trees. Mostly, I found beauty in the flowers, wild and so different from the vegetation that grew near my own home. In their singular brilliance, each offered me a lesson. The transformation that concludes the poem is, of course, also my own.

Gifts

And now, the islands' lessons come to me in flowers:

> From the frangipani, I learn choice—thirsty, it forms
> blossoms before leaves.

The hibiscus proves impermanence,
a single day breathing in its filmy folds,
while the honeysuckle holds out memory:
the subtle scent of a wrist, a breeze over open fields.

I learn boldness from the brazen bird-of-paradise—
its orange plumes and bright blue tongue;
from the lotus I learn love: what else
anchors in the mud, re-opens with the sun?

And the egrets in flight, trailing the hoe and plow,
they are a lesson in transformation—

wings white as paper; petals in the wind.

Coming to terms with my own history—as my great-grandfather's great-granddaughter, as a woman of Dutch descent, as a person raised in a hegemonic religious tradition, as a visiting academic—was a complicated process that spanned several years and multiple trips to Indonesia. It involved putting that journey into words, into poems. Arranging those poems into a series of lessons expanded my sense of history, of life story, of grace, and of embodied ways of knowing. As I write myself into greater understanding, the paradoxes continue in my life and my poems: that I bear responsibility and have the power to act, that the divine mystery occurs in many forms, that the intimate can be found in the distant, and that I can embrace discomfort and loss even as I learn from beauty and love.

Reference

Apol, L. (2018). *Nothing but the blood.* Michigan State University Press.

Pralini Naidoo

The tendency towards self-herding into rigid identity groups
more constrained and suspicious
a disconnect with our sovereign stories
a disconnect with earth, with mother tongues
with the mother wisdom

> that nurtures us and the wild places of our ancientness—
> an ancestry deep in time, place, and realm.

Vibrant—

Naidoo, P. (2022). Found poem from Joy in the dirt. In A. Fidyk, & D. St. Georges (Eds.), Poetic Inquiry for synchrony & love: A new order of gravity [Special Issue]. *Art|Research International: A Transdisciplinary Journal, 7*(2), 369-388.

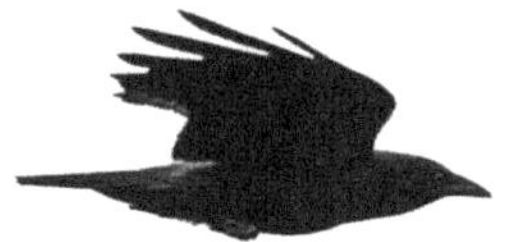

Ellyn Lyle & Celeste Snowber

Immersing to Re/Emerge: Living Poetically through Embodied Consciousness

Within living structures defined
by profit, by linear power, by institutional dehumanization,
our feelings were not meant to survive . . .
—Audre Lorde, 1934-1992

But they have.

Here, in a call for *poetic words* and *poetic images that honour the dynamic dimensions of the fullbreath of life* (Fidyk & St. Georges, 2022), we find space to *savour the sacred* even in *catastrophic times.* Like Audre Lorde, we understand that poetry is not an indulgence, but essential to our living and being. *It forms the quality of the light within which we predicate our hopes and dreams toward survival and change.* Poetry is where we turn to express those thoughts locked away in the corridors of minds, hearts, and bodies too long relegated to the periphery. In this way, poetry midwifes into the world our dreams for re/humanization.

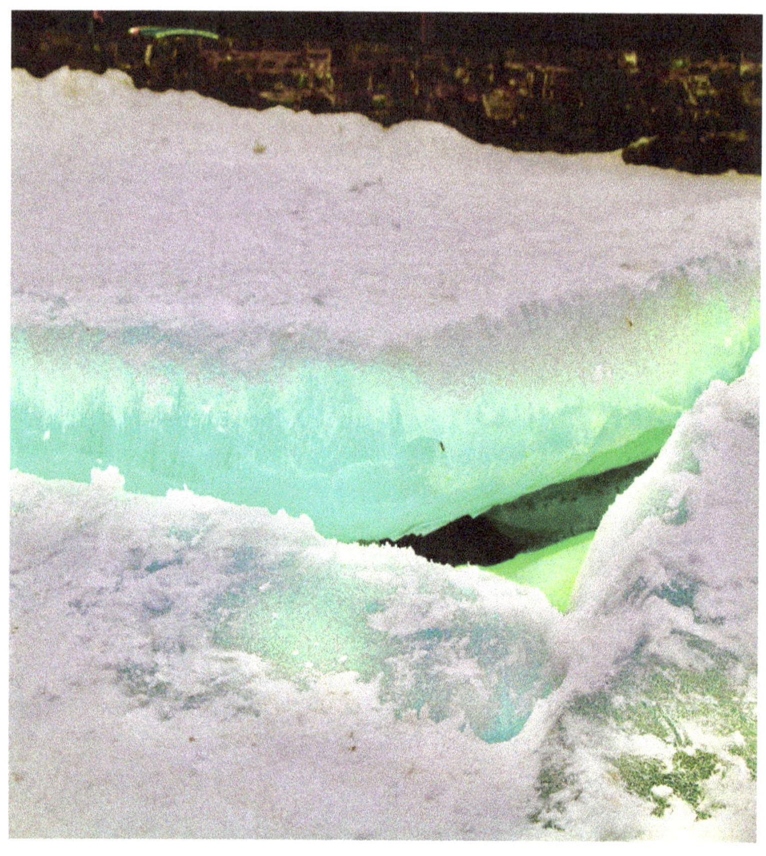

in the cracks and fissures
pockets of light
reminders of infinite potential
coalescing in re/membrances
of the divine with/in

With the world suffering the effects of multiple forms of *dis*-ease as evidenced in crises of health, racism, war, economic disparity, and climate vulnerability, we feel viscerally the need for healing. Finding hope in the synchrony of friendship and shared values, we engage photopoeisis to weave together poems and images that speak to our struggle to re/anchor compassionate consciousness in spaces that seem unmoored. Finding ourselves returning to our relationships with water as an expression of *bodyheartmind* cleansing, we explore how we immerse to re/emerge. We recognize the necessity of writing our renewal in a way that refuses to conform to the living structures of dehumanization that has made this baptism so critical. Thus, situating photopoeisis within post-qualitative inquiry

competing pressures

vying for pre-eminence

distracting from the
knowing within–

we are the wielders of power

the holders of hope

we are the possible

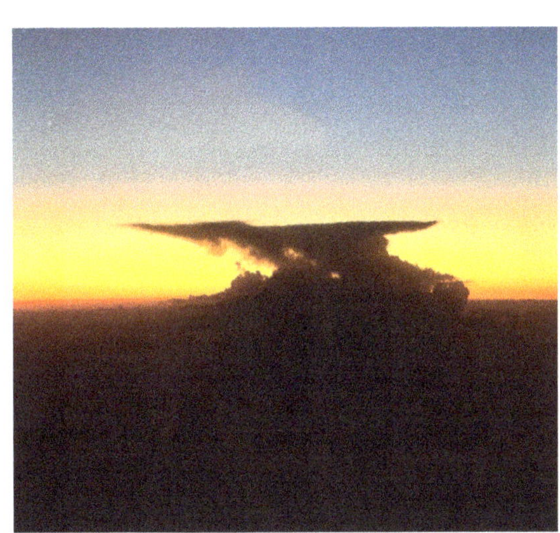

(St. Pierre, 2018, 2019), we find the courage to resist and reclaim. Like a glorious thunderhead emboldened by its water roots, we are determined to clear the air.

We recognize the risk we are taking. Systems long established push back when poked. Perhaps this is why Joanne Yoo (2019) and Graham Badley (2021) refer to this type of writing as *dangerous*. Made brave by their insistence that we must call out dominant discourse as deliberately constructed to prioritize *the ubiquitous* over *the embodied*, we re/centre *being human* in human being. We move forward with love and consciousness, "listening and acting upon the time to replenish" (Lyle & Snowber, 2022, p. 9).

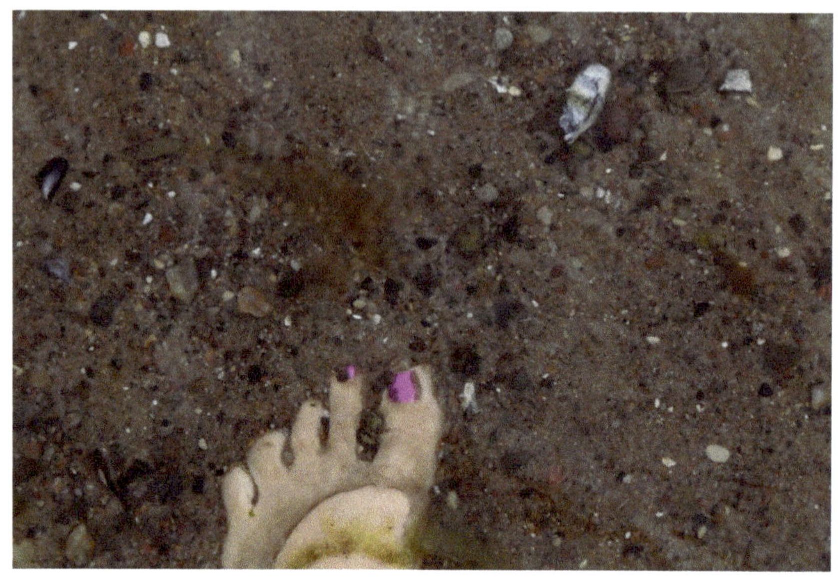

The body has a knowledge and wisdom
all to itself,
which is felt in the lived experience
of fingers and toes,
shoulders and hips,
through the heart of veins
and on the breath of limbs.

While we have become adept at engaging in personal rituals that buoy equanimity—what we understand as nurturing grace in challenging times—we recognize that more is required of us. It is not enough to find ways to energize so we can return to places of perpetual depletion; we must call out what erodes even as we work to cultivate new spaces that honour both our fierceness and fragility. We must enlist the courage to have conversations with others so that we insist on these re/humanized spaces each day, week, month so we may foster resilience in a world a drift.

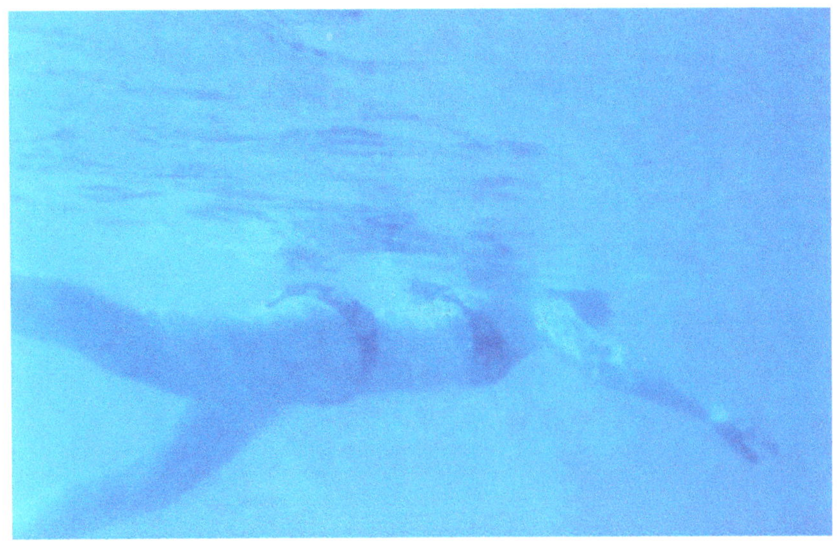

there is a place
    to undulate
front crawl, backstroke
        breaststroke
immersion
    sublime
        invitation to
oneness
baptism in a swimsuit

water becomes the medium
to know grace

Here, we find space to immerse and re/emerge. In being enveloped by the world's waters, we experience a rejuvenation of mind and spirit, just as the synovial and lymphatic fluids mobilize our joints and cleanse our inner seascapes. The buoyancy experienced in such baptism lessens the inflammation that hurts us and allows ease to permeate. Understanding the source of the *dis*-ease that we struggle to overcome as residing in structures of dehumanization, we return to Post-Qualitative Inquiry (PQI) with its focus on *living theories* that ask us to "follow the provocations that come from everywhere . . . [and] do the next thing, whatever it is—to experiment—and keep moving" (St. Pierre, 2018, pp. 603-5). Much as our bodies necessarily move with/in the water, the dynamic unpredictability of *always becoming* resists methodological enclosure. Instead, it demands curiosity and courage to dwell within an *ontology of immanance*. This fluid nature of PQI is what leads us to a new way of poetically framing the sacred nature of our relationships with water.

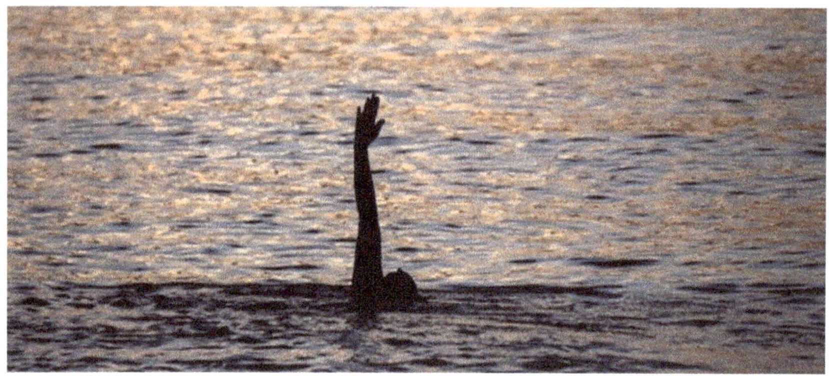

We are bodies born
of the same body

of water
carried by the tide to other harbours
perpetually called home
by the tangle of salt air and bated breath

souls buoyed by brininess
we immerse to re/emerge

—reborn

Photopoesis offers us a way of attuning to both wounds and wonder, permitting space for insights that may have otherwise been lost (Lyle & Snowber, 2021). It curates a living space of embodied consciousness that cannot help but to leave us transformed. LeGrange felt this, too, when he insisted "that method is performative," and we can choose to engage methods that make possible the transformation of the world" (2019, p. 8).

how many colours
        could one body

of water hold, change

        permutations in hues

swim into a festival
of light changing
            on the surface of you

fluid celebrations
saltspun off shore

      b r e a t h
            rises

                one more wash

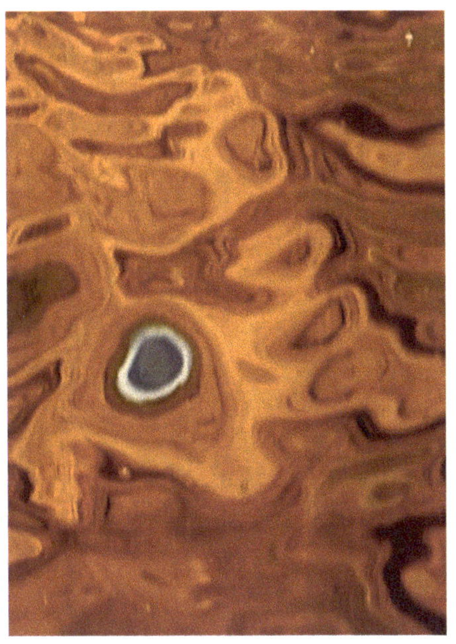

We recognize that this process of transformation is one that requires long-standing commitment. We acknowledge that we will need one more wash, again and again, as we seek cleansing to rid ourselves of what tries to cling so that we may resurface what matters—compassion, relationality, humanness. In seeking these ways of being, water matters as it helps us access through visual and visceral poetry our hopes for re/humanization. The presence of poetry in qualitative research is not new but it is often employed for its use to *represent* knowledge already held (Fackler, 2021; Faulkner, 2019; Leavy, 2015). Like Patricia Leavy, we engage with arts-informed ways of knowing not as representational, but as epistemological. Maybe this is what Carl Leggo (2005) meant when he advocated for *living poetically* . . . that in privileging "performative dimensions of languages, images, and gestures over their literal or representational ones" (Fackler, 2021, np), we would learn to un/privilege the historical tendency of academia to devalue art-full and embodied ways of knowing.

can one recalibrate
a path
        a trajectory?

is there a thermodynamics
        to the soul?

following the heat
of one's passion

change the pressure

        and flow

with what calls you

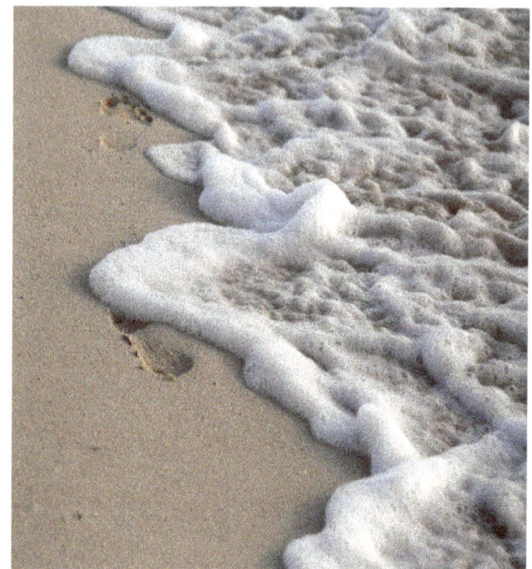

It is often easier to write about these principles that we value than it is to live into them. That is why we are drawn to the salt water in our lives—our tears, the sweat of our toil, and the sea. Here, where we are creatures of fluidity and change, we know our own vulnerability and resilience. We are called to stay porous—open to what may come and the potential to be transformed through loss, love, and listening deeply to our own lives. Through this place of an *ontology of immanence*, everything is within and without, deeply connected. In honouring the fluid nature of our lives, we learn to let go of *that which is* in favour of *that which is always becoming*. We hear and heed the invitation to relinquish that which no longer serves us so that we may re/emerge more buoyant.

one stroke
    in cerulean blue

holds a thousand shades
    grief, exasperation

to respire
    a whole surrender
water bares the weight

all in a morning
    release

Images

All photos by Ellyn Lyle, with permission.

References

Badley, G. F. (2021). We must write dangerously. *Qualitative Inquiry, 27*(6), 716-722. https://doi.org/10.1177/1077800420933306

Fackler, A. (2021) *Poetic inquiry* (screencast). https://qualpage.com/2021/12/23/poetic-inquiry/

Faulkner, S. (2019). *Poetic inquiry: Craft, method and practice.* Routledge.

Fidyk, A., & St. Georges, D. (2022). Editorial. Poetic Inquiry for synchrony & love: A new order of gravity [Special Issue]. *Art|Research International: A Transdisciplinary Journal, 7*(2), pp. ix-xv.

Leavy, P. (2015). *Method meets art: Art-based research practice.* The Guilford Press.

Leggo, C. (2005). The heart of pedagogy: On poetic knowing and living. *Teachers and Teaching, 11*(5), 439-455. doi.org/10.1080/13450600500238436

Lyle, E., & Snowber, C. (2022). Nesting with/in the bloom. In E. Lyle (Ed.) *Re/humanizing education* (pp. 1-9). Brill|Sense.

St. Pierre, E. A. (2018). Writing post qualitative inquiry. *Qualitative Inquiry, 24*(9), 603-608. doi.org/10.1177/1077800417734567

St. Pierre, E. A. (2019). Post qualitative inquiry in an ontology of immanence. *Qualitative Inquiry, 25*(1), 3-16. doi.org/10.1177/1077800418772634

Yoo, J. (2019). A year of writing 'dangerously': A narrative of hope. *New Writing, 16*(3), 353-362. doi.org.10.1080/14790726.2018.1520893

Daniela Elza

Putting Words Up to the Light[14]

Surfacing

suddenly   you cannot stop writing about
                                                                 the light in winter—

the canvases it throws   each day   on your walls—

you make cup   after cup of tea   seeking some path that aligns
with your focus
                    with your absence
                                                    with your universe—

                                                              hoping for small miracles.

nothing is squandered once you secure   *solitude.*

you stumbled along the shoreline that is   your heart—

14. There is a curious saying in the culture I was born in: *a person who sings does not think harmful or evil thoughts.* I think of poetry as a kind of singing, a kind of tuning in and paying attention. A deeper kind of listening and presence in a community of voices. How do we practice such attention in a culture of utter distractions, fragmentations, and alienations? Electronic devices now follow us anywhere and claim us, even when crossing a street. They re-wire our minds, alter our voice and divert our gaze away from our children. Attending deeply seems foreign in a twenty-four-hour news cycle. When we sing, it is the poetic devices that claim us. When we harmonised with each other, we tune into each other, into the connective tissue of nature, the creativity with which she whispers to our intuitions. More importantly it builds community. This grounds us, stabilizes us, puts us back together in a world which keeps throwing us off balance.

it's a view

it's a sound

it's a rock in the shoe.

these fragments—

glint off the surface of the ocean take off like birds.

how easy for us to become ordinary.

how we do what we must because we didn't do
what we should have.

yesterday it was the fog that engulfed the swaying boats the leaning trees—

you had no time to look for fancy words to chronicle this longing.

today the angle of the changing light

keeps you preoccupied.

makes you

extraordinary—

as if time were but/ a choreography//
of all that is but is/unseen and taking up//
residence in us/remembering itself.
—E. D. Blodgett, 2019

words did not dare

come in. this place where hold and touch command
their own lexicon and syntax

where all I can do   is listen with all my might.

regret   or guilt   bleed the body elsewhere.

here in the low cradle of the moon
with the crickets   in the late night garden
                                        under your gaze

in the arms of the waves   and crash of the surf
the body shifts
            gears
                speeds down its neural highways
                            studded with stars—

                    suddenly we are all fingertips
        neurons   ears   mouths   and tongues
leaning in like wind swept trees.

the second brain   drowns out   the first—
        these partisan interruptions
                                        speeches
the mind trumpets from its soapboxes
                        through its loudspeakers.

tonight the surf is   so loud   the scent so strong
        and this sensual dissent   is quiet—

mouth to mouth   we spell   its mystery.

here   the body sheds its sorrow   briefly
for a change   aches with   love   like that.

“And in the shadows of our human dream of falling
human voices are Creation’s most recent flowers,
mere buds of fire nodding on their stalks.”
—Li Young Lee, 2008

in the arc of falling

in the shadows
the song begins before thought—

a distant note grows
to a raging engine in the sky.

I had my suspicions.
this lying down with world

this tuning into the low pitch
hummm of the earth. plucking of
Creation's most recent flowers.

between us— no words yet
just *mere buds of fire*—
these volatile beginnings
of song.
nodding on their stalks— echoes
looping a winter sky
synaptic clouds
caught in the throats of guitars.

no chords of strained lyrics yet
no drumbeats of accusations.

just hanging around.
mucking about.
messing with the pro-
found.
such promiscuity leads me
thrills me.
sorry Joe.

this moment is. never having
enough. still more to say
even on my way out of town—

Split this Rock

write an opera   for a captive audience.
dozens of handcuffs jingling
                    chirping
                         like insects.
something of many   voices.

why poetry matters is   why peace matters
why having a normal life   matters.

scoop the body of the beloved   in your thoughts
and words.   *take the risk*
                  of the voice-walkers.

wend through numerous   false beginnings

to get past   the wardrobe   of a man
        without getting locked   in his eyes.

to get past   the police officer
      trigger quick   finger twitching

to get past   the cynical viewer
    the complacent listener
                  the stuffy commentator.
            the jets scraping the sky.
    or that pipeline   or why
we invaded another country—
you are always going to disappoint someone.

here we are   at the Lincoln memorial
            don't wear your hoodie today.

here we are at the cherry blossom festival
              don't wear your headdress.

here we are at the *poets against war*
take a photo with them.

and here we get it
wrong again
and again.

is astonishment enough?

to weave
a safety net for the heart?

to wrestle words out of the earth's mother tongue?

to recall that tune
you knew
how to hum?

to sing a song for unlocking handcuffs.[15]

References

Blodgett, E. D. (2019). *as if*, p. 38. University of Alberta Press.

Lee, L. (2008). *Behind my eyes*, p. 103. W. W. Norton & Company.

15. *Split this Rock* is a conference I attended in Washington DC in 2012. The italics, inspiration and some of the imagery came from the event.

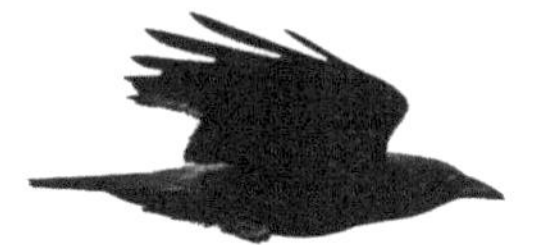

Lee Beavington

River in the Sky: The Fraser River Floods

Water

transparent as a miracle
you hold the oceans together
glue for body and blood

you trickle from cloud and kidney
pool invisible light—
diamonds in dark places

you ascend the tallest trees
dissolve mountains into memories
steep in planet-sized puddles

science calls you colourless—tasteless
yet you float, flow and freeze
keep DNA from falling apart

atmospheric river
the great giver
all life flows from you

but too much and we drown
like my grandfather—
his lungs swallowed you whole

November 15, 2021. The rain will not stop. The drive to downtown Victoria is like a roller coaster: adrenaline-inducing and out of my control. A turning lane runs like a river while geese swim above rotting pumpkins in a farmer's field. I park the car and wrangle the umbrella to cover my eight-year-old son and I. We stumble against the wind as rain pelts the street like water bullets. The sidewalk pay station, fully moated a foot deep, is beyond reach.

Inside Parkside Hotel my son watches the koi in the synthetic pond, its surface a calm contrast with the outer maelstrom. An occasional fish mouth bites the air. Like me, this controlled and stale environment forgets the external wildness. Until—during my son's appointment—I overhear the receptionist take call after call of cancellations. Sooke is shut down. Mill Bay is inaccessible. The Malahat Highway is closed. It feels like a disaster movie being acted out in real time and we're caught in the middle.

A few hours later, after the appointment, we step outside. The sky is sun and blue. More surreal than a Terry Gilliam film. Yet a gale-like wind lingers, a reminder of the atmospheric river that just passed through.

This is the day of the Fraser River Floods.

Fraser River Floods

Hell's Gate—never more furious
Highway 1 carved like butter
concrete dust and asphalt sediment
fill the beds where unborn salmon sleep

downstream
Aunt Nancy now owns a lakeside home.
Castle Fun Park moated inside and out.
Cows drown in barns—the lucky ones
sent for slaughter before the flood

upstream
bridge and rail strewn like broken toys
but transMountain pipeline is on schedule
stays the course on banks it breaks
carries secrets for us to burn

downstream
the muddy claw of the river's mouth
reaches for my island home
a plume of brown blood
Visible from seafloor.
Visible from space.

upstream
the quiet roar of staləẃ
remembers her body as glacier and rain
ever ready to run clouds to the sea
this fury of life—full of blessings
falling on deaf ears

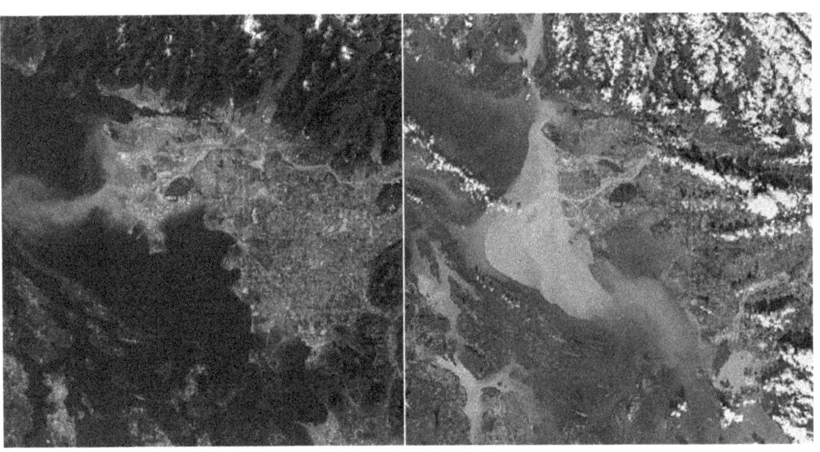

A Mouth in Flood. Satellite images show a typical plume from the staləẃ or Fraser River (left) and after the Fraser River Floods (right). The brown plume extends all the way to my home on SḴŦAḴ (Mayne Island).
Photo credit: Earth Observatory/NASA.

In Hope, a month's worth of rain falls in a single day. Nearly 300 millimeters. That's six times what parts of Egypt receive an *entire year.* Boats drive down the Trans-Canada Highway. Farmers refuse the evacuation orders to stay with their animals, only to have to abandon countless cows, pigs and chickens when water levels soar. Mudslides trap more than 300 people in their cars, where they spend two hair-raising nights before being airlifted to safety. The entire city of Merritt is evacuated. The cost in damages? 7.5 billion dollars. The cost of life is even higher: more than 640,000 farm animals (Chaya, 2021) are taken by the waters.

With a group of colleagues at Kwantlen Polytechnic University and the Kwantlen First Nation, I'm co-developing a staləẃ (Fraser River) field school. Living on a Gulf Island, I've never considered this place to be connected to the staləẃ/Fraser. A few days after the floods, I pass Miner's Bay on SḴȽAḴ (Mayne Island). The usual clear waters are inundated with debris; an entire cedar lays in the ocean, branches and roots rocking with the waves. How much of this came all the way from the staləẃ?

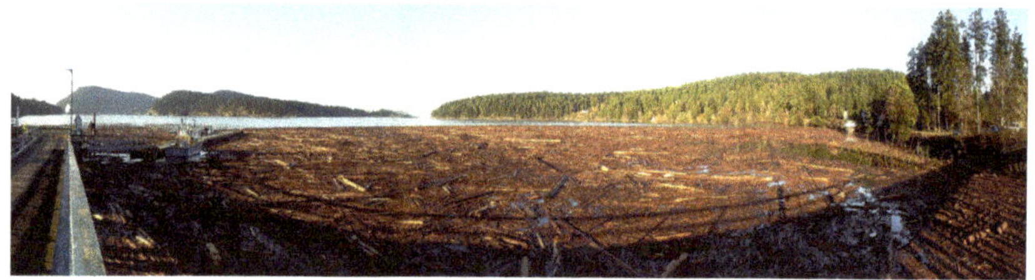

Bay of Debris. Miner's Bay on Mayne Island after the BC Floods. This bay is usually clear. Photo credit: Lee Beavington.

This serves as a wake-up call. I feel as though we have ignored the river's plight, and so she flew above us to ensure we heard her message. The Fraser, Pacific Ocean, salmon, my grandfather—we are all connected in a web of relationships. In a physical sense (we all share minerals), an ecological sense (we all feed from water and land) and a spiritual sense (we are all part of a reciprocal animate cosmology).

These floods caused unimaginable harm to hundreds of thousands. The death and destruction can't be described by numbers alone. Yet such tragedy and hardship can also be times of transition and re-prioritization. Consumerism and affluence hold little meaning during disasters. What truly matters in life? How are we contributing to the climate crisis and what can we do to mitigate this? How can we respect the power of the river?

I am a scholar-settler of European ancestry. I live on the unceded and traditional territories of the Coast Salish peoples. The Fraser River, named after a Scotsman that barely survived her waters, has existed for at least 10,000 years. Many Indigenous peoples, including the Coast Salish, Dakelh, St'át'im, Okanagan, Secwepemc, Tsilhqot'in, and Nlaka'pamux have deep and abiding connections to the staləẃ? (the Kwantlen word for river, what we now call the Fraser). This includes transport, trade, fishing, hunting, ceremony and spiritual practices. Settlers continue to threaten this way of life. These Indigenous peoples are the original river keepers, the ones with stories of her sacred waters that stretch back for generations. Someday, hopefully not too late, the namesake of this magnificent river will return to the Indigenous peoples.

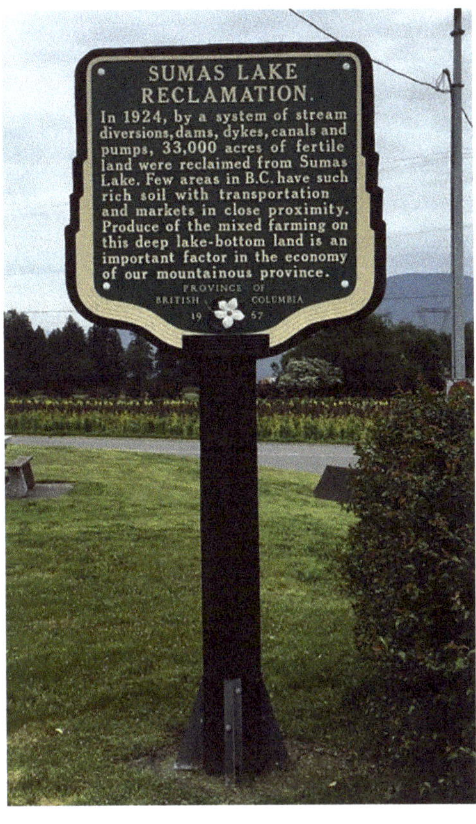

Sumas Lake Reclamation. A heritage plaque in desperate need of decolonization.
Photo from readtheplaque.com.

These floods also resurfaced a memory of a lake lost to colonization (Reimer, 2018). Sumas Valley was not a valley until white settlers decided to "redeem" this land (see heritage plaque image). They didn't want the annual floods, the mosquitoes, the shifting seasonality, and gave little to no thought of the Sema:th that had lived and thrived in reciprocity with Sumas Lake for millennia. A hundred years ago this lake was drained, and only now do many realize what was lost.

Lost Lake

the heritage sign reads:
33,000 acres of fertile land

reclaimed from Sumas Lake
birthed 10,000 years ago
your waters now stolen

some tell how the Sema:th
fished your wonders from cedar canoe
built homes on stilts to escape Mosquito.

These stories are in the water
each end is a beginning.

Barrow the settler had a vision:
to farm the floodplains
but first,
he had a lake to murder.

an entire ecosystem to suck dry
the fish left to die
they gasped for days.
how many dreams of tadpole drowned?

These stories are thin ice
one wrong step and you sink.

vested by the power of God
and dredgers and dykes—
we moved a river
drained a lake
extracted Sto:lo's heart
like a fetus from the womb.

These stories are here to stay
a century-old scar.

one day, Sumas Lake, you will be remade
when the Barrowtown pumps fail
and we are gone

forty-eight hours is all it will take
for sturgeon to sing you home

References

Chaya, L. (2021, December 3). B.C. floods: Livestock death toll reaches 640,000 animals and counting. National Post. https://nationalpost.com/news/canada/b-c-floods-livestock-death-toll-reaches-640000-animals-and-counting

The Fraser Basin Council. (2013). Bridge between nations: A history of First Nations in the Fraser River basin. https://www.fraserbasin.bc.ca/_Library/Ab_NonAb_Relations/bridge_between_nations.pdf

Oliver, J. (2019). Settlers coveted Sumas Lake. The British Columbia Review. https://thebcreview.ca/2019/07/03/572-settlers-coveted-sumas-lake/

Reimer, C. (2018). *Before we lost the lake: A natural and human history of Sumas Valley*. Caitlin Press.

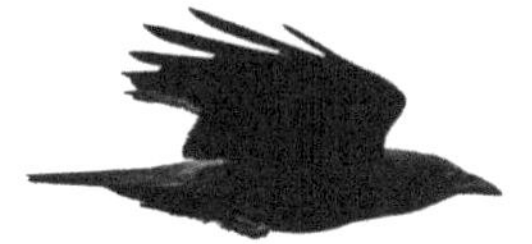

Ruth Vinz

The weight of absence became us
inside and beyond us
endless longing

Absence saturated everything.

It opened spaces of longing
his face like a hologram
my brother in the black irises of my mother's eyes

Presences in the absences too.

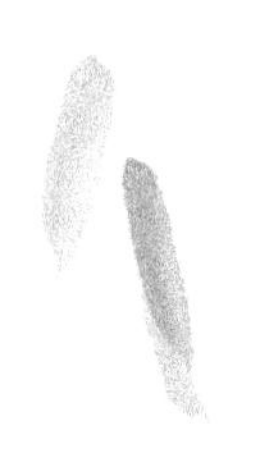

Vinz, R. (2022). Found poem from (In)habitings. In A. Fidyk, & D. St. Georges (Eds.), Poetic Inquiry for synchrony & love: A new order of gravity [Special Issue]. *Art|Research International: A Transdisciplinary Journal*, *7*(2), 389-413.

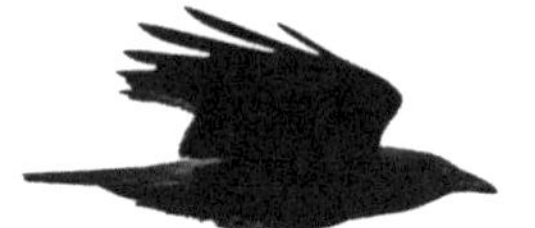

Jackie Seidel

We Were Here

Spruce Trout River Owl Stars Wasp Pine Mice
Fly Moss Dragonfly Squirrel Eagle Moon Creek
Swan Bear Sun Chickadee Mosquito Cougar Bat
Bluebird Bobcat Bumblebee Human Wolf
Poplar Wind Crow Moose Microbes Fox Deer Skunk

And all the Rest
Who depend on this Rocky Mountain
Glacial melt
Heaven
Have gone to
Hell.

Their chorus asks what is a watershed when we are all gone when we are all gone when we are all gone but who hears a tree falling in a forest? I can tell you for certain now, that koans are true. One hand is also clapping. It sounds like death. Its applause is quiet and loud and deafening and silent. It sounds like climate chaos biodiversity loss extinction. Where are the insects? Where are the birds? Where are the bees? Did anyone see where Grizzly Bear went?

What is this lung burning firesmoke choking darkness hot winds now every fucking summer? This is connected to that. But in his response letter, the government minister who has never loved this watershed mansplains that the owls will benefit because mice will thrive in the new environment and the owls will have more to eat. It's a done deal, he says.

Because jobs claps the hand. Because jobs.

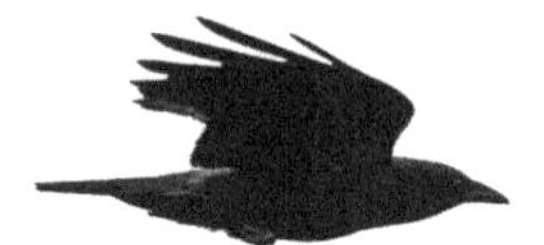

Stephen Levine

Love Words

Love. Caught. Entrapped? Let me go, lover.

Like flies to salamanders, I am tongued to thee. Words surround. Countless, they count. Resound. In this petty pace. Time, gentle man. You and I.

Maker, poet, pot-stirrer. Auscultations abbreviated endlessly. Appropriated. Own voice. Do I? Very well, then. I salute thee.

Salutations, sister! Left-handed. Caught and trapped. To be eaten later.

Do I dare? After all is said undone. Only sound. Resound. Echoes in the hallways. Antechambers. Strait the gate. None who dare to enter there. None my name. *Ouden*. Escape the trap by writing (not).

I see you seeing me. Read me? See me? Touch, feel me? I am (not) real. Bites and bits. Agenbite. Chew on that and spit out spite. Dim-wit. None can see who art not blind. Who art. Researching again. Again. Again. *Com*-pulsion. Spitting out words. Waste. Shame of sham.

To make real by writing. The word opens the door. To you? To truth? Silly, putty! *Putain. Moi. La meme chose*. I choose to right the world.

In the cave light a candle. The writing on the wall. Mene mene over and over again.

Along came a wind. Begin again. There is no end.

The end.

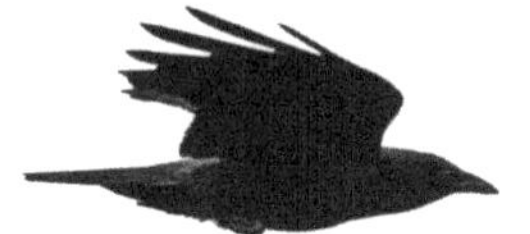

Jodi Latremouille

As Your Heart Breaks Open

I have no words…

I sit in front of a blank page
three days running
running scared

John Welwood (1992) has words. He says:

In opening our experience
to life as it is,
we often find
that it does not meet
our expectations
of what it should be.
Perhaps we don't fit the picture in our mind
of who we should be.
Perhaps those we love
don't measure up
to our ideals.
Or we find the state of the world
disappointing,

Credit: Reprinted from Latremouille, J. (2022). Grief-writing: Navigating ecological suffering through a relational pedagogy. In A. Fidyk, & D. St. Georges (Eds.), Poetic Inquiry for synchrony & love: A new order of gravity [Special Issue]. *Art|Research International: A Transdisciplinary Journal*, *7*(2), 439-457.

even shocking.
Reality is continually breaking
our heart
by not living up
to how we would like it to be.
(p. 169)

three days running
running scared
no salvaged words emerge
for this worldly, wordy and stubbornly wilful

educational reality

imposed/

composed
deposed/

reposed/

exposed

protective shell, cracked

Yet the heart itself cannot actually break,
for its very nature is soft and open.
What breaks open when we see things as they are
is the protective shell
of ego-identity
we have built around ourselves
in order to avoid feeling pain.
When the heart breaks out of this shell,
we feel quite raw and vulnerable.
Yet this is also the beginning
of feeling real compassion
for ourselves
and others.
(John Welwood, 1992, p. 169)

my heart breaks open

for the younger ones
who languish through the door:

"I'm late,"

"I'm hungry,"

"I could really use a nap."

and… it's only first period.

Robert Bly (1926), in his poem,
Advice from the Geese,
has honking words:

Hurry! The world is not going to get better.
Do what you want to do now.
The Prologue is over.
Not a stitch can be taken on your quilt
unless you study.
(n.p).

I have no words…

my heart is breaking
for those older ones with the wide, bright smiles,
waiting at the door:

"Welcome!"

"Nice to see you!"

"Here, take this granola bar,
you seem like you could use it-
split it with your neighbour,
it's my last one."

The page is still blank
I have no words
For the

educational/

vocational/

taxational/

pre-occupational/

sensational

bittersweet perplexity

inadequacy

impossibility

Wendell Berry (1983) has words. He says:

There is no one to teach young people
but older people,
and so the older people must do it.
that they do not know enough to do it,
that they have never been
smart enough
or experienced enough
or good enough to do it;
does not matter.
they must do it
because there is no one else
to do it.
(p. 84)

I have no words…

my heart is swelling
for those older ones who are never

never good enough
never smart enough
never experienced enough

the only ones
the courageous ones
waiting
smiling at the door

Feeling our "broken-open-heart" has a bittersweet quality.
Reality never quite fits our fond hopes-
that is the bitter taste.
The sweetness is that when reality breaks our heart,
it is calling on us

to soften and open.

As we soften and expand,
we discover a sweet,
raw tenderness

toward ourselves

and the fragile beauty

of life as a
whole.
(John Welwood, 1992, p. 169)

breaking that too-tiny, too-sweet granola bar,
breaking it out into
miniature morsels
doling it out
stretching it out, pulling it out into
tiny pieces of…

enough

just enough

as your heart breaks open there will be room for the world to heal.
(Joanna Macy, 1996, p. 175)

open,

soften,

expand

a tiny chocolate chip, salvaged from the wrapper
on the tip of a finger

one single,

good

question

melts on the tongue,
spreads,
softly sighing

sweet,
sweet
sal(i)vation

raw,

fragile,

whole.

References

Berry, W. (1983). The loss of the university. In *Home economics: Fourteen essays* (pp. 76-97). Counterpoint.

Bly, R. (1926). *Advice from the geese.* Poets.org. http://www.poets.org/poetsorg/poem/advice-geese.

Welwood, J. (1992). The healing power of unconditional presence. In John Welwood (Ed.), *Ordinary magic: Everyday life as spiritual path* (p. 169). Shambhala.

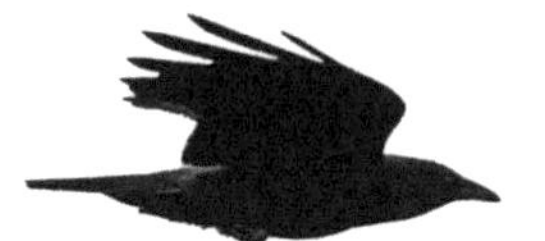

Addyson Frattura

In this moment I am halted. Maybe I am thrown.

I attend to being seen into existence
the existential fear of becoming

Language and self and other act as
    glimpses
    anticipations
    attempts

at finding and opening a doorway
an invitation to another—

Poetry holds hurt in its line breaks
in what is left absent and lingering

A poem is meant to break.

Frattura, A. (2022). Found poem from Where does it hurt? In A. Fidyk, & D. St. Georges (Eds.), Poetic Inquiry for synchrony & love: A new order of gravity [Special Issue]. *Art|Research International: A Transdisciplinary Journal*, *7*(2), 477-496.

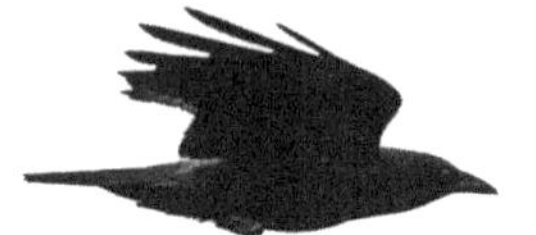

Nancy Halifax and Sheila Stewart

a poetics of unlearning: an inquiry into unsettling white settler colonialism

> the quantum physicists have it right; they are beginning to think like Indians;
> everything is connected dynamically at an intimate level.
> —Joy Harjo, *Conflict for holy beings*

setting : Halifax Art Gallery

Characters
smith
Jones

prologomena : our intent

smith
[lights cigarette \ takes a deep drag]

this's not curative
here's uncertainty
the contestation of master narratives
a re-orientation from the normative task of assumin' a consensual interpretation

our breath : imagines : troubles
whiteness
we're white
we're here
to empty the white nation state

its legislation
its declarations
its deprivations

canada : meaning : unbearable

Jones
[stepping forward]

unbearable

Habit

ritual habitual
hiding riding
my rocking horse

hot in my
green & plaid skirt
hear the clock slow

down
get loud

—what am I doing
in the next

century—

wind

smith
[poplar trees shiver]

the next century
begin in the folds of middle seeking comfort or hunger or a map
begin by drawin' uncertain lines 'round language

& i don't forget the others i'll draw lines for them
i'll begin : bein' accountable
no : stop not like countin'
unless the count is tender

i'll begin : with white rationality white fear white theft
yes : i'll begin
& against this i'll draw a never knowing shitty hope filled body

remember : no one wants ~~to feel~~
boiling water advisories
empty language apologies
mercury dumpin' ~~see appendix for unremediated toxic crimes~~

Jones
[with blanket]

toxic apologies I am sorry
sorry ashamed I ask
God's forgiveness

If I write about my father

he will reach up
from his grave, grab
my ankle, drag me down, stuff
dirt in my mouth, gouge out
my eyes.

But he had his ashes
interred in an Irish village so I will burn
in hell alone in the colonies, the new
world not new, my ashes will be
dumped in a dumpster.

No one will

sprinkle them on the white
gravel of that plot where
my parents lie, Presbyterian
to the bone.

No one will stir

my dust into the St. Lawrence, let
moving water bathe and let me
go—

Why do I imagine myself without
release?

I am not barren

land. I am
landed misplace
placed settler

unsettled
writing my father.

(lift back blanket)

interlude : greed

smith

we have all the things that [are]
admired the great powers

sky

[lighting dims]
Jones

what am I doing in the next century—

writing snagged on the past

cloth   clothes   robes   academic gown caught
on door handle   remains of a church pew

wool blanket covers

grief

smith

[lights down \ almost dark]

covers   language   :

\ covers what i broke \ stole \ excluded

severed from   skin   land

created   n a t i o n c i t i z e n a c t s   to deny   murderous   tongues

interlude   :   greed

terra nullius
no history of colonialism

anguish

Jones

my entry point to language

language
l/anguish
anguish

a foreign anguish
english…
— M. Philip NourbeSe

enter my language
my language point

enter language
my language's entry

language my entry
enter centre

enter *ma langue*
point to you my centre my enter

my language anguish
my lang   lang lang

ma langue ma langue
ma langue's hot tong

ma famillé ne parle pas français
moi, non plus

mais j'aime la langue

European languages
anguish

my entry point

bone

smith
[moving forward. centre stage]

my entry \ pointed breakin' \ broken

i cannot leave you there   broken   lost
so i will be here in this place
with tears   & the exhaustion of not knowing
& knowing not

i'll write   unsettle the security of Nations
draw a line & rejoice
"the Pentagon claim: poetry presents a special risk to national security"

i'll chant stories   call spirits call animals call rivers
invoke a carefilled singing
in solidarity   conjunctions refuse to be swords

i'll write refusals
pray

smith

we exist between dream & earth
we're drawing a world that illustrates an end

to order

we conjure a world

conjure justice   know integrity   know hunger   conjure love
know poverty   know racism   know ableism   conjure fairness
know shame   know   conjure

prayer

Jones

never barren

never barren land   never
empty

never empty

wool blanket: how did you come here— a ship a plane

English sheep
factory sleep

what we try on:
headdress in front of a tepee

Indian Crafts in my father's photo album labeled us *Irish Indians Ancient Irish Tribe of Mohawks*

uncovering the racism in my family
centres my whiteness I don't want to re-inscribe it
Father making album album making
him us

who is our archive what do we wash over
curriculum we were fed

who makes it through school
to university
what happens there
there-them-us

the pleasure of our pocket knives & whittling make-believe
games pouches
hanging from our pant loops we were enthralled by "Indians"

my first boyfriend was ....adopted into a white family his brother
to another family

personal colonial-church-missionary

hearing my father preach about the tragedy
of the "Third World" I wanted to go there
see for myself get away

I don't want to appropriate
but I need to pray

your creator yours   not mine

my god was never mine
my lineage eating yours

lichen pond worm

smith

your lineage eating mine

alive's a sort of roughness
nibbling & clutching   at my intent
moving along celestial banks
a contagion
a rehearsal of exhaustion
a gathering of arms
the scourge of your caress

caress

Jones

If I write about being a settler
it'll sound fake
other settlers will squirm
Indigenous people will leave
people will think I'm trying to look good
not be racist
not be seen as racist

if I don't unpack being a settler
think only about
yoga   breath
kindness

no

kindness

Jones

smith

this is not the end
this is accountability
this is love
this is uncertain
this is what implicates us
this is unsettled
this is a question
this is land   a wound   inadequate
this is writing   a worlding
this is a prayer   fatigue   failure
this is what we have

with love

birth

in 2019, we (smith & Jones) first arranged & performed this piece at the international poetic inquiry symposium at the halifax art gallery. the symposium theme was established in response to the united nations year of indigenous languages.

we revisited it early spring 2022. our poetic arrangement articulates a kind of feelingknowing that supports us to imagine differently: different collectivities, different selves within & beyond nation states. in our performance we address how canada only recently admitted (albeit with a great deal of ambiguity & lack of action) responsibility for the genocide of indigenous peoples & nations. calls from the state whether they are to attend to indigenous languages, truth & reconciliation, or to indigenize curriculum, are insufficient. our performance counters a reinscription of colonial values through its commitment to imagination & imaginations's capacity to disrupt taken-for-granted genealogies of feelingthought, & "ways of reproducing the world around [white] bodies" (Ahmed, 2013).

References

Ahmed, S. (2013, September 11). *Making Feminist Points.* https://feministkilljoys.com/2013/09/11/making-feminist-points/

Butler, J. (2010). *Frames of war.* Verso.

Harjo, J. (2017). *Conflict for holy beings.* W. W. Norton.

Philip, M. N. (1989). *She tries her tongue, her silence softly breaks.* Ragweed Press.

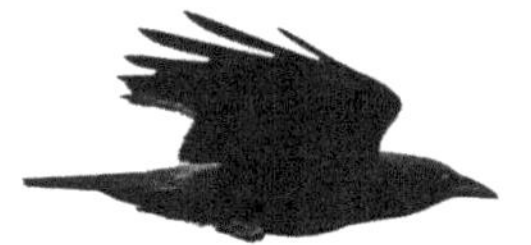

Lee Beavington

My children playing in a forest no longer there.

The land now strewn
with tree bodies
there is room to topple the final Cedar in one fell swoop

Thumping the ground, Her body reverberates
naked trunk a skeletal wisp

Shock is all that remains.

A grief too great to bear
Gone now, the deer, creek, and fern—

To learn respect for life and place, must we first cause harm?

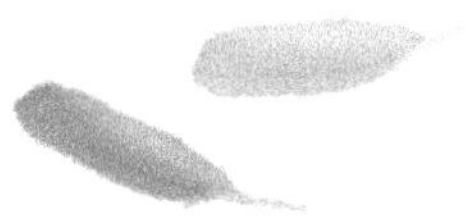

Beavington, L. (2022). Found poem from Snow in summer. In A. Fidyk, & D. St. Georges (Eds.), Poetic Inquiry for synchrony & love: A new order of gravity [Special Issue]. *Art|Research International: A Transdisciplinary Journal*, *7*(2), 519-541

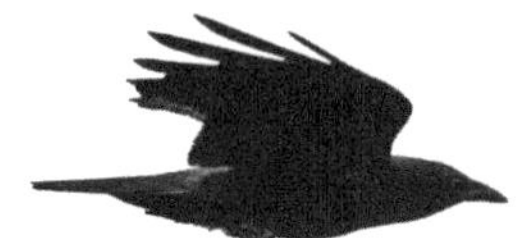

Kedrick James

A Bird Sanitarium

Who said coots are crazy?
Is it not crazier to hatch a nut to
make a spoon of bills
to pipe in sand
to have painted your head red to
make a ruff star linger
to have a puff to rob a rave in to
be a lover of peas for a fee
to suck sap until your belly yellows
to shear water with a foot of flesh
to skew a polar south like a sniper
to leach petrol from a storm
to swallow a barn on the sagebrush savannah or
swallow a bank, a cliff, a cave, or a tree
to catch flies with ash in your throat
and hum with Calliope as you surf on cows to tattle on a
wandering cinnamon teal
to tern elegant and black and royal as a sandwich?
Is it not crazier to have bridled a mouse to a tit to
turn a stone black with the wag of a tail
to make wings with cedar wax
to peck the ladder backed with wood
and choose between greater or lesser yellow legs?

And is it not crazier to be bitter in America to be a bewitcher of the DOW
to be bunting indigo snow with a bat
to cover your back in canvas and chat

with a Mexican chick? Well, *a dee dee declare*! Is it not crazier for a razor to turn the Troggs on or for the Big Dipper to crow for fish
to pin a tail on a duck, or morning on a dove?

Is it not crazier to coo at the cook
lewd as a cur, long in the bill but golden-cheeked
now that war's a blur and hooded red-faced hermits cross bills with cranes on a hill of sand
to fall for a con artist selling the prairie
and slide olive-sided down the pacific slope to grackle with a boat on your tail

to Iceland, laughing, mewling, gullible
to scrub Florida while smoking a Mexican jay dark-eyed, strung out like a kite
with long spurs lapping at the land,
or go fishing for kings with a belt?

Is it not crazier to try to outwit god with a golden eye
or goose the emperor cackling in the snow?
And are you not crazier than a common loon to
kill a deer for a horny lark with your limp kin to
make a cracker with nuts
to drink screech with a fowl whiskered elf
and brown a pelican pie in a pewee bird oven
to put Montezuma on a scale and gambel with quail to
run across the road flexing pectoral pipes
until you're spotted cruising on white winged scooter
down the ridgeway rail?

Is it not crazier to stork hearts of stars in your throat to
soar above the beardless tyrannulet
while lucifer hums in your white ear drinking
parasitic Jaeger-bombs
with Merlin until Mag (num num) pie-eyed starlings
free their bushes, tits, and boobies
and run on black-necked stilts
to a magic house in the cactus canyon and is
it not crazier to willet to be so?

To catch gnats and wind up with a gross beak
to snipe at aliens on whimbrel
to hawk your tricoloured Heron eBay
to play solitaire for a long-toed stint
at the end of town only to sing swift vespers
with the Mighty Sparrow and travel wild Turkey
with a flame-colored tanager
in a summer dress that thrashed the scarlet poll red
blessed by a Bishop bruised black and blue
a cock taking coca too, riding th' rush
mocking a bird whose fantasee mutates
to chat with a Cardinal who richly knew
the best of the rest of the birds that flew
to roost erstwhile with a fella on the rope
face a cool pink amid the flaming goo
was the madly handsome curly curlew.

Earthshattering

The accidents of birds, & a temporal blindness,
—-that any can escape
the brutality of the past—as if!
The persecution of matter, no water
well wishes until we embrace all beings' equality, by which I mean everything,
birds and the trees in 'em, barnacles and the whales on 'em.
Here, where Humility commits suicide,
and hubris drives by in a Jag
splashing muddy water on thin skinned shadows of Humanity, we'll
make nests
a bed of Earth-sickness and drown, thirsty among the stars.
The reality of television,
of a meaty following,
of some dingleberry doxa,
of that gilded cistern
in which we piss and take stock of the wind lest we be left
wet legged!

I hold up a finger to find a breeze
on which I might catch a ride back to Buddhism.
By the time it comes it is too late, and Religion sickens me.
I grow my hatred of the Host
like a dry beard, and blow smoke in
the eyes of the Righteous,
who never solve the mysteries
of a violent death, clasp it like penitents in prayer. The
cycle of life crushes on,
and
I leave no trace in its wake.
The Fall erupts with hindsight.
The eternal bewilderment looks
dashing as a clam.
My fingers are computer-tipped, and I breach in earnest, seeing for
the first time my anitbody,

dressed as a digital chauffeur,
            coming toward me
                        threateningly.
I cast spells to ward it off, the canaries of
my conscious mirth stop singing

And I imagine myself blessed!
I am as normal as Drought's shadow.

Then you show up, homing pigeon in hand, wings
akimbo and all higgledy-piggledy
suggesting a trip in a time machine bound for Bethesda, hoping to
best the battle drones
            with a sick disco dictaphone ringtone.
    Cassettes come in handy, strip and trigger an EMP
with the hopefuls and awfuls, the handcuffs and microphones, a diet
of daily media mountebank bathroom blowouts, jobs,
a newsfeed of peanuts for pay.
Art arches her aching backgammon game plan, puts a
tile on the dignitaries' spike
            and is bounced to the back of the line
dancing when the turns stop coming around.

It's-not-over-yets filling the flower vase lit
with wilting degrees, 4 of them,
sanctioning the perfunctory shutdown—50 years of
sequels to the wailing babe and still no hits!
Enough of this, the careers in advertising masquerading as a solemn art.
            Ads take over
cancel our subscriptions to the resurrection of circular thinking.
Instead, sold this
common plastic pomegranate
and the rebirth of wool and bistros. Baaaa baaa solo in
the bruised
and gruesome jazz minted from akashic records,
                        all the blue notes,
            coconut semen sunscreen slathered

over by bolero and guaguanco, as if the conquest
of the Waldorf Astoria tripped on Amerigo Vespucci's washboard and
was sufficient to predict the Violent Femmes.

Little brown jug don't I love thee, a post-apocalyptic jingle. Truth be
told, we should have seen it coming,
the hooplas and the Sunkist fancy dancers, caterers
holding court-martials, dressing in the gallant
hats of conquistadors with some idiot movie star
presiding like the Beast over the Judgement
of the All-might-be, and none the wiser for it.

Darlene St. Georges

Ruby

beautiful throat
belligerent pink
light up dark cascades
with volumes of discourse—
a sonnet of hashed memories

flickering   fluent

carried on winds into caverns
magnetizing fissures—
subtle forms
prima materia
your intimate core

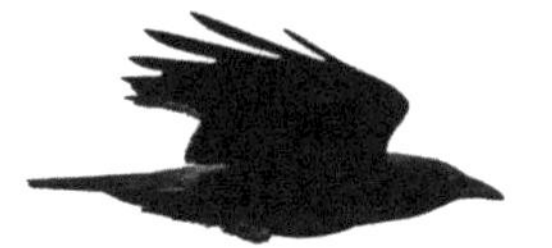

Tessa Parent

Boy and his Beast: A Tale of Healing and Belonging

Red Woman hadn't been to see Boy in three days. Beast was back to his old self, pacing the perimeter, snarling at anyone who came near. It was worse than before—now Boy knew what he was missing. He used to tell himself he didn't need anyone. Now, he missed catching frogs with Little Girl. She had taught him how to hold gently so he could feel their hearts fluttering, cool skin against the palm of his hand. And he missed exploring with Freckle Boy, who taught him songs to sing as they marched through the forest. He tried to sing now but Beast's howling was too loud, and Boy couldn't find his voice. And, most of all, he missed the circle with Others, where there was ceremony, laughter, and storytelling.

Before Red Woman came, Beast kept Boy safe. Boy had only a fuzzy memory of the Darkness: the feeling of electricity jolting through his belly out to his fingers and toes, yet being frozen in place. He'd collapsed into himself, while the Darkness set upon him.[16] Much later, he awakened curled up against Beast's belly, his tail draped

[16] This story is an extended metaphor of the lived experience of a boy who lives with trauma. Because trauma hijacks us in the moment, we often withdraw, isolate, and live apart—causing lack of the very thing that can bring healing—friendship, love, and caring relations. When something triggers the body's memory of trauma, often a mis-read threat, Boy fragments, dissociates, freezes, and or collapses. These states correspond to self-protective responses: fight, flight, freeze, and collapse. When our autonomic nervous system (ANS) is overwhelmed, we typically fragment or dissociate from our core—our somatic centre of being and subjectivity. At this point of the story, trauma is left vague purposefully: the reader creates their own interpretation so that an identification can happen. That is, some of us may have interpersonal trauma—neglect or betrayal for example—some of us may have inescapable death trauma as during a motor accident or severe illness. Trauma herein is understood not as an event but the response to an event—it is a subjective experience, "a rupture of one's sense of self," one's internal organizing narrative (Lombardi & Gordon, 2014, p. 179). When we experience a rupture to self, we often lose trust in the spirit and or natural order of a place. Further, "Boy" as the protagonist's name, following in the tradition of folk tales, enables the listener to identify with the character and unfolding plot. In a similar way, time and place left unspecific invites further projection of particulars by the reader. We do not

over Boy, keeping him warm as Beast licked Boy's wounds. After that, when the Darkness came again, Beast leaped into a rage, snarling and baring his teeth until it retreated. The last time had been long, long ago, yet Beast still wouldn't let Others near Boy. Once, Little Girl had come too close, wanting Boy to play, and Beast had pounced upon her. Boy had tried to hold him back, but he was too powerful. Little Girl, sobbing, ran back to Others. They didn't let the children near Boy after that. Others gave Boy food, but they approached cautiously and retreated quickly. They whispered "He needs to learn to control it is all. He could if he wanted to."[17]

Red Woman was the only one who was not afraid of Beast. When she came the first time, Beast attacked with his full ferocity. She just sat down. She didn't say anything, just sat with Boy all day. "I'll be here when you're ready. I'm not going anywhere."

The next day, Beast did his best to chase her off, gnashing his teeth and roaring his deafening roar. She just sat again, a little closer. "I'll be here when you're ready. I'm not going anywhere."

Day after day, she came back and sat with Boy. Slowly, Beast stopped trying to scare her off. One day, Beast lay down and drifted off, breathing soft and slow. Boy cautiously eyed the woman, noticing the red glow that emanated from her.[18] She opened her arms and Boy crawled into her lap, let his head rest against her shoulder, her glow enveloping him like thick warm honey. He sank into sleep, deeper than he had ever known. When he awoke, she asked, "Are you ready for a lesson?"

need to know details of a person's trauma in order to act with empathy. In order to build resilience—the capacity to deal with the inevitable adversity life brings—we must have trust that the world is basically a good place (Poole Heller, 2019, p. 31). When we understand the nature of trauma, our young people are more likely to be met with empathy and support, building trust that their world is basically good.

17. Unfortunately, children are often punished for what Porges (Embodied Philosophy, 2019) suggests is largely beyond their control; a hypervigilant defense system mistakenly detects a threat, so the child reacts in a way that's considered inappropriate and is subsequently punished.

18. Red Woman's "glow" represents her energy, presence, and non-verbal attunement. Jennings (2019) suggests that a child who has suffered trauma may pay too much attention to the other's mood and non-verbal cues—which may have been more important than spoken words in surviving traumatic environments—subsequently missing key verbal cues in other environments (pp. 33-34). Understanding this phenomenon may allow adults to approach the child with support, rather than punishing him for not paying attention. Moreover, adults may see the importance of ensuring they practice self-care in order to show up for children emotionally regulated and present—ensuring they do not distract the child who is so acutely tuned in to others' mood and energy.

Every day she taught him something new. They walked and talked and breathed and stretched and stitched and read and cried and wrote and prayed and sculpted and drummed and drew and visualized and planned and sat and reflected.[19] Quiet at first, Boy began to talk, sharing little pieces of his memories. Red Woman listened and nodded and glowed. Beast followed them, but he kept his distance, content to watch from afar. He slept a lot. Some of the children joined them—Red Woman's glow dissolved their fear of Boy. They ran and played and climbed and dug and built and collected and painted and braided and planted and harvested and laughed and hugged and looked and listened.[20]

One day Red Woman said, "Are you ready to join Circle?" Boy glanced at Beast. He was laying on his back, head rolled to the side, snoring softly in a patch of sunlight. "Ok," said Boy. They walked toward the circle, and the Others shifted over, making a space. Red Woman smiled at them, sat down, and patted the space beside her.[21] Boy sat close, safe in her glow. As the chatter and laughter spread around the circle, Boy noticed Red Woman's glow, seeping out, enveloping the Others one by one. As it did, they looked at him, smiled, and one passed him a dish. Salty goodness melted in his mouth and a warmth settled in his full belly.[22]

19. From therapeutic benefits, to meaning making, to communication, art can allow an avenue for self-expression, exploring identity, and processing trauma abstractly (Rhoades, 2018, pp. 66-68).

20. These activities help Boy heal, but they are not exclusively for him: all the children participate and benefit. Though art can be used specifically to support marginalized and traumatized children, it will benefit any child, identified in these categories or not (Rhoades, 2018, p. 66). Coleman (nd) further supports the arts as both a method of healing from trauma and for promoting resilience through their therapeutic value as expression through non-verbal communication (p. 6). At best, most children will enjoy the activity, and in the worst cases, of trauma, the arts are "particularly useful in communicating about things for which there are often no words" (Malchiodi, cited in Coleman, nd, p. 12).

21. Red Woman's glow represents a higher self, one who has done the inner work to check her ego and love others unconditionally. It is Red for the root chakra: it emanates safety, security, and belonging. She is regarded highly by the others; they trust her enough to allow this Boy—a threat of fragmentation of their group identity—a chance in their community.

22. Though Boy has experienced trauma, the community is intact. It has access to resources. One of the reasons Boy is able to heal is because the community has the resources to meet everyone's needs. Saul (2014) addresses the way that loss of resources can exacerbate collective trauma (p. 5). Attig (2011) describes the loss of a loved one as a tear in the web of connections that help form one's sense of identity. In a similar analogy, Erickson (1976) describes the Buffalo creek flood as snapping the threads of the social fabric. Relating to others is how we find meaning and purpose. Though Boy's trauma is purposely vague, whatever it was, he alone experienced it; the Others' ties remain intact, so Red Woman is able to weave him in.

In Circle, the Others sang and swayed and danced and beat drums and held hands. They cooked and told stories and laughed and cried and prayed. Boy felt bubbling up through his chest and neck, tears filling his eyes. He had never felt a part of something before.[23] He was part of Circle: his voice adding to the music, his feet stepping in time. Red Woman's glow was brightest then, and each of the Others glowed too. Boy felt a hum in his bones: he was safe here; he belonged here.

One day, when they were playing with the other children, Freckle Boy held him down. It was part of the game; he'd been captured and was their prisoner now. But Boy was scared; the Darkness flashed in his mind. Beast came barreling through the brush, crashing into the clearing, roaring and snarling and tossing Freckly Boy through the air. Beast stood over Boy, reared up to his full height, towering over the terrified children as he let out a deep, earth-shaking bellow. The children scrambled away, screaming in terror. When Red Woman came Beast flashed his teeth with a deep, menacing growl, inches from her face. She paid him no mind, and picked Boy up, cradling him in her arms, and as her glow soothed him and his heart slowed, so too did Beast's. She carried Boy back to Circle and rocked him. The Others came close and their bodies told Boy *you are bad, go away, we don't want you,* but Red Woman told them, "Hush," and rocked Boy to sleep.[24] When he woke, she had spread her glow to the Others, and their bodies once again welcomed him.

But now Red Woman was gone. Some of the Others had tried to come help Boy, but Beast snarled at them and they were frightened off. If only they would wait a little longer - Beast would tire out if only they would wait. But it was too late. The red glow had washed away, and Boy sat cold and alone. Beast had paced and clawed in a frenzy until there was a trench around them.[25] Day after day, he heard singing coming from Circle; he nestled deeper into Beast's fur until everything was dark and quiet.

23. Clark (2016) suggests connection and working through trauma with the arts, movement, ritual, and ceremony, rather than pathologizing and labeling. Red intersectionality sees trauma-informed practice as reinforcing colonial practices of pathologizing, labeling, and medicating—perpetuating powerlessness (Clark, 2016). Boy's healing comes in part from learning to trust the safety of Red Woman's presence, attunement, and care, experiencing acceptance by the larger community, and participating in healing practices. He—his being and behaviour—is not labeled or pathologized.

24. The non-verbal communication of the Others causes a physical sensation of shame in Boy's body—telling him he IS bad. Red Woman's intervention prevents this from becoming a shame cycle. See Stokes and Lewis (2018) for discussion of shame and shame cycles.

25. Anger or inconsistent responsiveness to an infant's distress or bids for attention may lead to the infant spending more time in an alarmed state, eventually developing chronic hypervigilance. The child may later overreact and respond to non-threatening situations as

When Red Woman finally returned, Beast did his worst to keep her out. She ignored him, as usual, and said "I'm sorry that happened to you," pulling Boy into her glow. She explained she'd left to spend some time taming her own beast. "You have a beast?" asked Boy, wide-eyed. "But I've never seen it, where is it?" he asked, looking around. "She's always with me, but usually she stays back, watching. Every so often she rears up and I must tend to her. She is trying to protect me; I must reassure her that I am safe. Only then can I return."

Years later as Boy marched through the forest, singing songs with Freckle Boy and some other children, they spotted someone, curled up in a hollow in the side of the ravine. Creeping closer, Boy saw it was a small girl. Her face was ashen and lifeless; she looked like she had been here a long time. Boy touched her gently on her shoulder. She rolled over, blinking slowly, then as she registered him her eyes widened in terror "No! You have to go now! Run!" Before he could reply, a thundering roar came from above, and a monstrous shadow loomed over him. As the thing lunged toward him, orange eyes flashing and yellow teeth bared, its acrid, putrid breath choked Boy's lungs, making him heave and wretch. The children screamed and fled in terror. Boy's belly dropped, his chest seized as his heart pounded and electricity jolted through his limbs, ready to run. As he watched the girl plead and sob, trying to hold the thing back, Boy heard Beast stirring, his hackles raised, his teeth bared, letting out a warning growl. But he felt something else. Boy hugged his arms around his body and took slow deep breaths; a red glow emanating from his heart.[26] Beast sat down, alert but curious, enveloped in Boy's red glow. As the terrible thing snarled and stomped about, Boy sat down beside the girl, letting the glow wash over her.[27] "I'll be here when you're ready. I'm not going anywhere."

threatening; thus, his hypervigilance reinforces unintegrated, internal perception of self and misinterpretations of the intentions of others (Jennings, 2019, p. 19).

26. Porges suggests creating a feeling of safety in the body by cueing neuroception triggers for trust and safety, which will override the physiological state of defensiveness on which anxiety rests (Embodied Philosophy, 2019). Porges explains that the cause of our anxiety which triggers neuroception is beyond our awareness, but evident in our bodies. Techniques described by Levine for creating a feeling of safety such as the self-hug, tapping, and squeezing muscles help to orient the body as the container for sensations and feelings (NICABM, 2017).

27. Boy did not ask for his trauma. He did not need it nor create it for some "life lesson for spiritual growth." Yet Saul points to prevailing with increased competence, resources, or believing something good came out of a traumatic event, as a component of resilience (Saul, 2014, p. 8). Boy's ability to check his ego, and witness this girl show the benefits that came with healing his trauma.

References

Attig, T. (2011). *How we grieve. Relearning the world*, pp. 128-162. Oxford University Press.

Clark, N. (2016). Red intersectionality and violence-informed witnessing praxis with Indigenous girls. *Girlhood Studies, 9*(2), 46-64.

Coleman, K. (n.d.). *Coping with childhood trauma: Art as a policy strategy.* Policy Brief No. 5. Institute for the Study of International Development.

Colman, A. (1995). *Up from scapegoating. Awakening consciousness in groups*, pp. ix-20. Chiron Publications.

Embodied Philosophy. (2019, August 5). Polyvagal Theory on Feeling Safe YouTube [Video]. https://youtu.be/hOZJn3XKw1s

Erickson, K. (1976). Loss of communality at Buffalo Creek. *American Journal of Psychiatry, 133*(3), 302-305.

Jennings, P. A. (2019). *The trauma-sensitive classroom: Building resilience with compassionate teaching.* Norton.

Lombardi, K. L., & Gordon, A. (2014). Life after "death": An empirical and clinical perspective on trauma. In M. O'Loughlin & M. Charles (Eds.). *Fragments of trauma and the social production of suffering: Trauma, history, and memory* (pp. 169-184). Rowman & Littlefield Publishers.

NICABM. (2017, June 2). Treating trauma: 2 ways to help clients feel safe, with Peter Levine. [Video]. Youtube. https://youtu.be/G7zAsealyFA

Poole Heller, D. (2019). *The power of attachment: How to create deep and lasting intimate relationships.* Sounds True.

Rhoades, M. (2018). LGBTQ trauma + art education. In A. D. Hunter, D. Heise, & B. H. Johns (Eds.), *Art for children experiencing psychological trauma: A Guide for art educators and school-based professionals* (pp. 60-75). Routledge.

Saul, J. (2014). *Collective trauma, collective healing: Promoting community resilience in the aftermath of disaster.* Routledge.

Stokes, S., & Lewis, S. (2018). *The trauma of shame and the making of the self.* Sage Publishing.

Barbara Bickel

Beholding the Unexpected: A Trance-Based Poetic Inquiry

Dreaming crosses boundaries of space and time, whether personal, political, historical or spiritual. As an artist/researcher/teacher I engage trance-based inquiry as an awake-dream practice. I have come to understand and trust this experience as a form of spiritual activism (Anzaldúa, 2015) and slow activism (Heim, 2003). It allows me to cross boundaries and to enter the unfamiliar, the unknown.[28] Trance-based inquiry connects me with what lives below the surface, with what is more than me. This inquiry took me to a place of compassionate witnessing of the historical pain and fear in the hearts of American people in the present. The pain felt very relevant to the current lives of Americans as the country was heading into a highly polarized and fear-filled presidential election. It led to a public performance of a Woman calling out for the holding of memorial space, of witness, of *wit(h)ness*[29] and care for the plight of others while she was being cared for, carried by and restored by the elements of sun and water.

The Franklin D. Roosevelt Memorial (FDR) in Washington DC was the location of this trance-based inquiry and performance. I often engage with trance-based inquiry *in situ,* in particular places, as a place-based inquiry, but I have never practiced it while in the presence of memorial art or with the intention to respond and inquire with and through art made by other artists. This trance-based inquiry experience took place prior to undertaking any research on the monument. I later learned it was designed by Lawrence Halprin and includes sculptures and artworks by five artists: Leonard Baskin, Neil Estern, Robert Graham, Thomas Hardy, and George Segal.

28. To learn more about trance-based inquiry see my 2020 book entitled *Art, Ritual and Trance-Based Inquiry: Arational Learning in an Irrational World.*

29. An Ettingerian matrixial word coined by artist, theorist, psychoanalyst and activist Bracha L. Ettinger (1999).

A few days after I entered my trance-based inquiry at the memorial, I performed the resulting poetic inquiry creation as part of the American Educational Research Association conference, and specifically in an Arts and Performing Inquiry Special Interest Group session, that took place at the memorial site.[30] I understand my poetic writing sourced by trance as an "involuntary poem," as the awake-dream does not always make sense to me when it arrives or as I transcribe it. The poem evolves later from "seemingly divided or unfamiliar parts, or even discarded ones, [dreaming itself] into a more complex, interconnected whole" (States, 1997, p. 32).

Engaging the Trance-Based and Poetic Inquiry

On a cool but sunny day on April 16, 2016, I walk slowly through the FDR memorial. I stop part way through the meandering outdoor rooms and passageways and sit in front of one of the fountains on the cement ground, sheltered from the wind (see Figure 1). I close my eyes and enter the awake-dream, I speak aloud and record my journey. I am aware of voices and footsteps nearby and allow them to lull me more deeply into the trance. When the awake-dream journey comes to an end I stand up and retrace my steps out of the memorial. I return to my hostel room and transcribe my recorded voice and from there an involuntary poem unfolds.

A few days later on a sunny but very windy and cold day, I perform my poetic inquiry. I stand atop a cement bench with the fountain visible behind me. In the midst of performing, I am taken aback by a passionate and emotional energy that does not feel like my own. It flows through me and carries my breaking voice on the wind, circling those watching the performance as well as tourists walking by.

After all the performances are over, I return to the fountain where I had undertaken the trance and continue my walk through the rest of the memorial. A surprise meeting takes place on the other side of the fountain in the next open-air room. I am greeted by a bronze statue of the outspoken First Lady, Eleanor Roosevelt—the first Chair of the Presidential Commission on the Status of Women, and the first Chair of the United Nations Commission of Human rights, made by the sculptor Neil Estern. Eleanor is notably the only First Lady depicted in a presidential memorial and it honours her role in the formation of the United Nations. My wondering about who 'she' was who appeared in my trance-based inquiry and performance, is answered.

30. The session was entitled *Response Ability*, organized and documented by Dr. Joe Norris. To see the on-site poetic performance at the FDR Memorial go to http://www.joenorris-playbuilding.ca/?page_id=1764

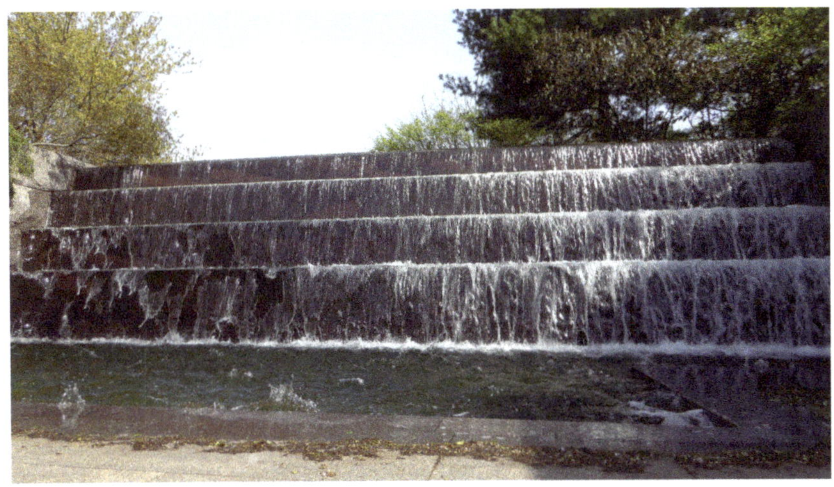

Franklin D. Roosevelt Memorial, Washington, DC, 2016. Photo credit: Barbara Bickel.

Beholden

She sits at the fountain in the sun convalescing
convalescing
convalescing

Her convalescences
enter the water
enter into water
warmed by the sun

Warm water transports her
behind the waterfall and
she
sits
watching people
through the waterflow

Through the flow of water
she witnesses the people
witnesses all the people
the wounded people

people tired
people hurting
people crying
people grieving
people worrying
people searching
people trying
all the people

All the people

people right where they are
people right where they should be
people tired
people angry
people sad
people searching
people wanting
people desiring
people knowing

She witnesses all the people

people working
people not working
people lost
people found
people so afraid

The people so afraid
people so not knowing
people so afraid

And she watches
she listens
she witnesses
she wit(h) nesses

she watches
she wit(h) nesses

and she watches
she watches
she watches people playing
she watches people exploring
she watches people looking

Looking and wondering
wondering and questioning
questioning questioning questioning
questioning why
questioning why why why why whyyyyyyy

From behind the powerful streaming water
behind the permeable wall
she holds them
holds them all

Holds them in her gaze
carries them in her heart
she carries them
holds them

She holds them
beholden beholden people

Know we are beholden

She thanks the fountain for holding her
at the center
allowing her to look out
look upon
look with
her people

She slides back into the water
surfaces at the edge of the fountain
lays on the ledge
sun dries her
hmmmmm

She curls up
convalesced

Acknowledgements

With gratitude to poet Dr. Marna Hauk, my roommate at the hostel during the conference, who gifted me with wise poetic feedback in the writing process, which took place within a very short time frame to be ready for the performance.

References

Anzaldúa, G. E. (2015). Flights of the imagination. In A. Keating (Ed.), *Light in the dark/Luz en lo oscuro: Rewriting identity, spirituality, reality* (pp. 23-46). Duke University Press.

Ettinger, B. L. (1999). Traumatic wit(h)ness-thing and matrixial co/in-habit(u)ating. *Parallax, 5*(1), 89-98.

Heim, W. (2003). Slow activism: Homelands, love and the lightbulb. *The Sociological Review, 51*(2), 183-202.

States, B. (1997). *Seeing in the dark: Reflections on dreams and dreaming.* Yale University Press.

Alexandra Fidyk

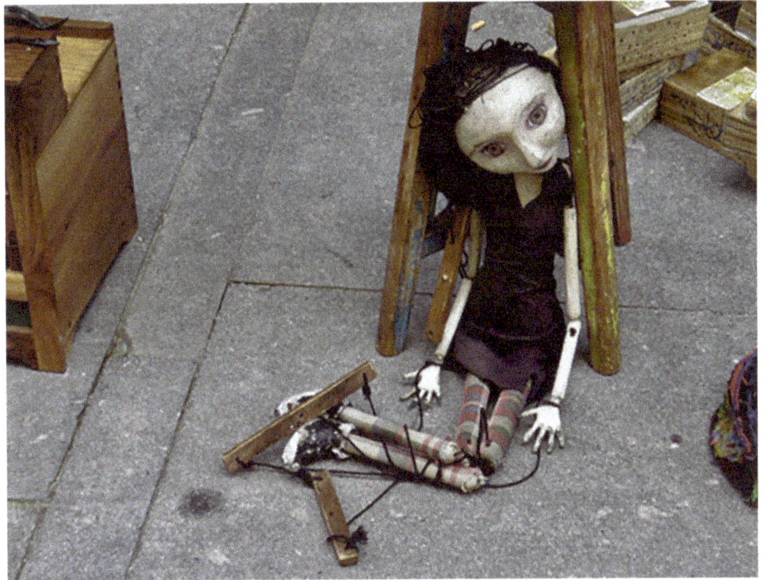

Marionette on street, Sintra, Portugal, 2019. Photo credit: Lisa Nackan.©

Becoming Eve

You expect me to submit
forget my animal root
lie down, play dead, surrender.

Bear your seed but abandon
my rhythm, my voice
my core, my truth.

What shall I trade for the
denial of Self and her sisters
Rage, Betrayal and Humiliation?

To succumb is to agree
to the fall, the split, the loss
Motherline—

as if She never was.

Sarah MacKenzie-Dawson

Burdened arrival
caught in an ontological chasm
a different understanding
entangled within layers
   opening the heart—

the lifeworld where meaning is perception first reason second.

   Poetry is relational.

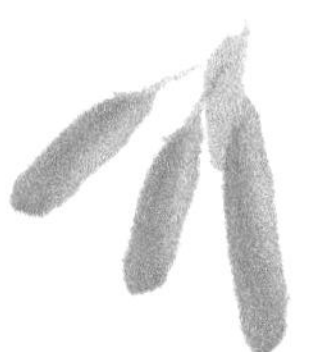

MacKenzie-Dawson, S. (2022). Found poem from A Review of *Doing Poetic Inquiry* by Helen Owton. In A. Fidyk, & D. St. Georges (Eds.), Poetic Inquiry for synchrony & love: A new order of gravity [Special Issue]. *Art|Research International: A Transdisciplinary Journal*, *7*(2), 543-553.

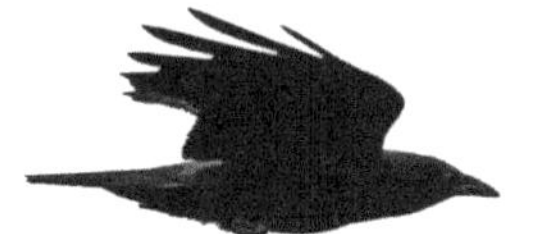

Ginette Paris

Heartbreak is an Archetypal Experience: William's Story

Denial

We know that abused children easily dissociate, in order to *not see and not feel* that the parent from whom they expect love and protection is the one inflicting harm on them. True to the definition of a *defense mechanism*, William's dissociation protects him for a while; he talks about Laura's betrayal as if it were just a little bump in the road. At the beginning of a break in a crucial relationship, denial and dissociation are to be expected.

Too big to fail

On Monday, when Laura left for work, my first thought was that she had met someone on that business trip to London. I could not help committing the indiscretion of opening her computer and reading her emails. She must have forgotten that I know her password, or maybe she just could not imagine how revealing was her sudden sexual coolness.

The emails revealed it all: my rival is Jeremy, whom I know, because we both train at the same gym. I read the email she sent him last night when I was in the shower, just before we made love. I also saw the pictures of their romance in London. It is so naïve, it can't be serious: love after a brief romantic escapade? I can forgive a summer fling! It is not a pleasant thing, but affairs happen. She'll come back to me.

The next phase for William is what a clinician would describe as a maniacal episode, a typical reaction to the initial shock of heartbreak. The phases can overlap, there is not fixed order in which they appear, but usually, a heartbreak raises *all* the defenses mechanisms ever listed in psychology.

Maniacal Obsession

William can't let go of his hope for Laura's return, a hope that is his worst enemy. Hope makes him live in the future, while detachment can happen only in the present.[31] *Hope makes William strategize obsessively; he fires one email after another as if his eloquent pleas could win Laura back. He states his innocence, appeals for her clemency, begs for a second chance.*

I am Hooked on Hope

Laura has moved out of my house; she rented her own apartment to "sort out her feelings" which, to me, simply means that she wants to be with Jeremy. I check my emails obsessively, longing, deprived, sad, filled with the hope that this sorting out will end with a sweet contrite email: "Jeremy is a big mistake, it's you I love, I am coming home."

I can't even go the grocery store without thinking I might miss her call, her visit. I fear Laura is choosing Jeremy over me and it sends me spinning in fear. Each time I panic, I send her another email. Every day, I spend hours crafting long eloquent pleas, and Laura answers back with falsely sweet and short replies, like: "Thanks for your lovely email. I need time and space. I hope you are taking good care of your precious self."

As long as William holds the belief that the return of the partner is the only way out of his misery, he remains hooked on hope. The psychosomatic consequences of his mania begin to add up and William soon shows symptoms of heart arrhythmia that make him feel caught in a labyrinth, a universal symbol for the emotional disorientation due to a sudden loss. In a labyrinth, every path leads to a dead end.

31. The French philosopher Andre Comte-Sponville (2002) writes beautifully about the danger of living with the wrong kind of hope. He wrote a *Treatise on Despair and Bliss!* (*Traité du Désespoir et de la Béatitude*) to argue his point.

A Rat in the Labyrinth

For the past two months, I have been feeling like a rat in a labyrinth, trying every trick to get the food pellets and not getting any. Laura keeps repeating that she still loves me, although she admits that she is also attracted to Jeremy. In this, she is honest, and does not deny sleeping with Jeremy. I beg her to tell me if I am still an option. She can't or won't answer; she remains ambivalent.

I remain in a daze; slow to feel, slow to think, hobbling haltingly from one necessary task to another, but with a heart beating too fast. I get food, eat food, digest food. I wash dishes, do my work, put my body to bed, and obliterate every thought or feeling. I am slowly progressing toward emotional catatonia.

My imagination is stuck in the hope of receiving even a crumb of love from Laura. I am trying, as my friends advise me, to "take care of myself." There is only one person in the whole world that can take care of me: Laura, but I have lost access to that person.

What is Love? I don't know anymore; I am utterly confused. I used to believe human love was the highest form of spirituality, and now it feels like the cruelest lie. I have experienced love as a great spasm of pleasure, an exclamation of joy, a physical and spiritual high, and now that same love in my heart feels like a tumor, a cancerous growth, a force that keeps me in bondage.

If love is not bondage, how can I explain that, after six months of her coldness, I am still, hoping, waiting for Laura to come back to me?

Learning about love's dark side

William's experience of the dark side of love belongs to the very nature of the sentiment. We are all agnostic (i.e. unknowing) when it comes to the mysterious nature of love. How could we not be?

Throughout all times, love has been symbolized by many things and their opposites: a cradle and a coffin; an initiation and a blinding; a lotus blooming in the heart and an arrow piercing it; a school of mystery and a torture; a spiritual discipline, a sport, an entertainment, a game, a war, a form of hygiene, a divine rapture.

It has been said that human love is pure/dirty, angelic/diabolical, divine/evil. It is described as the most intense *physical* experience, the basic *psychological* experience, and the most *spiritual* experience. It is felt as a blessing and a curse, a remedy and a sickness, a pair of handcuffs and a pair of wings, a glorious aura and a rope around the neck, an elevation of the heart and a falling down.

The contradictory nature of love is the truth of love

To expect only the angelic side of love is part of the immaturity for which heartbreak is a cure. The many contradictory symbols express what Jung called the necessary *tension of the opposites,* a tension that can either tear us apart or propel us to individuate.

As William's tension keeps mounting, so does his panic and physical symptoms. This is the point where William is most love-crazy, as if nature were pushing him to hurry up and make that *evolutionary jump.* William is usually a rational person, a professor of geography who just defended his second Ph.D., this one in psychology. He is not a young naïve lover, not a beginner, not a pathological co-dependent. Before his marriage to the mother of his daughters, William had been involved with four other women, with whom he had had strong erotic connections. Those relationships eventually faded and turned into friendships.

After his divorce, he remained a responsible father for his three daughters, even as he began the passionate relationship with Laura. Until the breakup with Laura, William had always been the one to terminate a relationship. The erotic attraction to Laura was his most sexually intense experience and the heat of that passion amplified his unconscious associations about his needs and fears. At the peak of his panic, William began to *introvert,* which means to turn one's attention to what is happening in the psyche.

What do you do with what was done to you?

As a depth psychologist, I ask *how* rather than *why*. For example, with William I would ask: "*how* do you equate the loss of Laura with a death sentence? How, when, in what form do you feel that you cannot live without her love. Give me examples, show me a body position that expresses your longing, tell me which songs make you cry." Once I have a good picture of the *how*, it is usually ripe for the next question: "Could you compare *how* the fear of losing Laura fits your earlier experience of having been neglected by your mother? What was your mother's *style of relating*? *How* does it resemble what is happening now with Laura?"

As William begins talking about his mother, we look at the similarity between his mother and Laura not as a cause but rather as a style of relating, one that he learned in infancy and includes a sense of having to beg for love. In that exploration of the style of relating (which is a how) William discovers something surprising which is that the terror of his mother's indifference could only resurface if a woman turned cold toward him, as Laura is now doing. Laura is giving him the cold shoulder in the same style as his mother. He understands that in all his previous relationships, until Laura, he had been the abandoner, *to avoid the terror of being the abandonee.*

Not long after the session where we explore his defense mechanism, William receives a package with Laura's name on it; he calls her and leaves a message on her cell phone to come and get her package. Receiving no answer for four days, he becomes worried and goes to her apartment to deliver the package and see if she is all right. Laura's apartment is a little studio built on top of the double garage of a large property and the staircase that leads to her entrance door offers a view on the bedroom window. William comes up the stairs, the blinds of the bedroom window are not completely drawn, and peeking through, he sees Jeremy soundly asleep beside Laura. A bunch of open suitcases and boxes are all over the bedroom floor, indicating without a doubt that Jeremy has moved in with Laura, a scene he had not anticipated.

Laura hears the footsteps on the stairs, sees William staring through the window, opens the front door, steps out on the porch, and closes the door behind her. She reacts with hostility to what she feels is an intrusion. Laura's hostile reaction sends William into the ultimate panic attack. The archetypal drama, like any story, has a turning point, and the following is William's most dramatic chapter.

Detach or die

I shall remember that morning all my life; she stood barefoot on the porch, barring the door as if I might have the intention of forcing my way in. I was bewildered by her hostility. She had not informed me that Jeremy had moved in with her, and there he was, suitcases and all. I began shivering from head to toe, feeling how she had again lied to me, a lie by omission but a lie nevertheless.

My heartbeat was out of control and my mouth was so dry I could barely swallow. I was standing in the doorway, shivering, silent and broken, handing her the package. Laura was emotionally cold, shut down, unaware that I was about to faint. She called my presence an "intrusion on her privacy, a crossing of her boundaries."

That was the language she had used many times to talk about her intrusive mother and her abusive father. Indeed, both her parents had repeatedly intruded on her privacy and really did not have psychic boundaries at all. But I had come out of concern for her, absolutely unaware that Jeremy had moved in. I had knocked on the door, I did not break in; I was not spying on her, I was delivering a package.

That cold hostile person in front of me was not the Laura I thought I knew, but the rebellious teenager she had described to me so many times, angry and forced to defend her autonomy against a controlling mother and an irresponsible alcoholic father.

The Laura in front of me was not my equal, not my friend, not somebody who could understand the vulnerable state I was in. She was the fragile, angry adolescent girl, incapable of seeing that I was somebody about to collapse on the floor. She asked me to "leave the premises immediately," but I was in no state to drive. I was having a panic attack, about to faint. I begged her to come sit with me in my car parked in her driveway, until my heartbeat went back to normal.

I don't remember in my whole life ever begging for a woman's compassion like I did that morning. I was five years old again, imploring my mother for help because I was burning with a 104-degree fever and thought I was dying. The coldness in Laura's eyes was just like the coldness in my mother's face when I disturbed one of her social events because I was sick, or needed something for class, or had to ask her for something, anything. Laura's lack of compassion for my obvious physical distress went through me like a sword.

She agreed curtly to follow me to my car, probably to avoid Jeremy seeing me. After a few minutes she expressed again that I should "respect her privacy" and "leave the premises" so she could go back inside to help Jeremy unpack! She said she did not owe me any explanation about her new situation with Jeremy. I left.

The most troubling emotion was not the experience of her utter lack of compassion; it was an uncanny physical sensation of being mistaken for somebody else. I had become like a member of her abusive family. Laura was reacting to her parents, not to the shivering, vulnerable, defeated ex-lover in front of her. She was not with me, not in our story; she was reacting to her past! And so was I, reacting the cold, aloof, ambivalent mother still living in my psyche.

The tension of this trauma was such that it created a "before" and an "after" and as such it was a useful turning point. Before this episode I was still confident that Laura and I could get over the crisis; but now, there is no more "us" and no more "we". I am hurting, but it is now clear that I am hurting alone. What is even clearer is that Laura's betrayal is just the top layer of my unfinished business with my mother.

Relationships are complicated and it is a fact that sexual infidelity often destroys them. But contrary to the dominant psycho-moral discourse, it is not necessarily the sexual nature of the betrayal that fractures the connection. Psychology is fond of hypersexualized theories about relationships.

William's traumatic experience was *not only* a reaction to seeing Laura in bed with Jeremy since he already knew about Laura's sexual affair. The shock was that of Laura's indifference to his distress. Feeling Laura's aloofness was the turning point in his recovery. From then on, as we shall see, he became an *agent* instead of a passive victim.

Of course, William can construct a narrative where the past experience with the mother *causes* his panic at Laura's aloofness. Since Freud, whose style of inquiry is that of a pipe-puffing detective trying to find the culprit, psychiatry has been mostly interested in finding the *causes* for all mental disorders. Parents, especially mothers, have been psychiatry's preferred culprits. "I am neurotic *because* mom and dad…" is the same kind of causal narrative that make scientific discoveries possible. It works fine with problems caused by an organic brain defect but fails when it comes to changing relational modes.

Except for those unhappy souls who remain stuck in infantile expectations, heartbreak often *needs to happen* for our lives to unfold in a positive direction. All relationships, without exception, contain a measure of unconscious tangles, more or less dangerous. Unraveling those threads is for William the turning point because it situates him in the present, and with options. William is now on the path to recovery. There is still some rocky territory ahead but he has pull himself out from the tar pit of passive suffering.

William is a turtle dying in its shell

Last night, having some regrets at the way she treated me when I delivered her package, Laura called me and suggested that we should have dinner together. Our separation was never quite final and although I have good days when my obsession with Laura is abating, there is still a part of me that remains hooked on hope. I was getting excited at the idea that she might tell me that having Jeremy move in with her was not a success.

So, after work, I went to the supermarket to get the ingredients to cook a gourmet dinner. I opened an exceptionally fine bottle of Burgundy, put flowers on the table, turned on music . . . everything was ready at six, but she arrived forty minutes late, distracted, dressed in jeans and a t-shirt, as if she had come from the gym. She gulped in exactly ten minutes the gourmet dinner that had taken me an hour to prepare, swallowing without tasting. Her eyes avoided mine, no relaxing into the experience of eating, no melting in each other's presence, as a good meal used to do for us. Why did she invite herself here? I felt she had come not because she really wanted to evaluate how things are between us, but because she felt guilty: she likes to think of herself as a compassionate being, a pacifist, and a loving soul. Laura adopts lost dogs and cats, feeds birds, plants trees; she participates in programs to heal the ocean, heal the forest, preserve wild horses, the rain forest, the ozone layer, aging elephants, panda babies, sick dolphins. She will not boil a live lobster and won't travel to China because they eat dogs and cats. She is a do-gooder who cannot face the fact that she betrayed me, lied to me, and lacked the most basic compassion when I was in shock at her door. Do-gooders can be the cruelest partners: they torture you with a saintly aura. I know that, but still, I had hope.

We had barely finished dinner when she got up to start the dishes (the Good Girl again.) When done, the good girl thanked me for the delicious dinner and said she really cared for me and hoped I was doing ok. Her pity was disgusting. Then she stabbed me with the kind of lies good girls will tell when they are unconscious of their dark side: "Excuse me, darling, I have an avalanche of emails to answer tonight. This was lovely, I loved seeing you, and it was important for me to re-establish our friendship. You know how much I love you and I would not want to hurt you. We don't know what the future of our relationship might hold. Let's remain friends. Now, I must get home early." I knew without a doubt that she was going straight to Jeremy. Laura's quick peck on my cheek at the doorstep felt like a slap in the face, a blow disguised as a kiss, her form of emotional lie. She left, probably feeling she was still a compassionate person because she had visited me tonight. Stupid me!

As soon as she left, I realized how utterly defeated I was; abandoned, rejected, unloved and unchosen, lied to, manipulated, and used, lonely and vulnerable.

I went to bed early, and woke up at 2:00 am thinking I was having a heart attack. I ended up at the hospital emergency room, and was told I was having "stress cardiomyopathy," in other words, a panic attack. I came home heavily sedated, to a cold nest.

That is when I got a powerful inner image: I am a turtle on its back, dying in its shell.

With the metaphor of the turtle dying in its shell, William found his location and although the image is painful, it is a crucial information. It tells him: "William, you are psychically dying. Get out of that shell immediately."

Abstract language, like "I feel lonely. I am cold. I have no appetite" don't give you much useful information whereas *I am a turtle turned on its back, dying within its shell* is *exactly* how William feels: a lonely turtle, turned upside down, trapped within its own shell, drying up, dying in isolation. His imagination opens up with this metaphor and the emotion is immense; it makes a difference in his body temperature. Finding the right image is an artistic activity that wakes him up and tells him his location. Among the infinite possibilities of images this one gave him an *emotional* understanding of the situation. As Bachelard suggests, a symbol puts the feelings *outside*, "as if they were images" so you can look at them as you would look at a painting. The image was saying: "William, your turtle is *dying*, this is serious! You need to reach out of your *turtled* self! William really *sees*, with new clarity, how he is psychically dying.

Academics make subtle distinctions between symbol (which may need interpreting) and metaphor (which doesn't). The logo for Apple computers is a tale with many versions, but the one that has meaning for most Christians is a reference to Eve taking a bite in the apple to participate in divine knowledge. Yet, for a non-Christian this icon may need interpreting. By contrast, a metaphor speaks directly to the unconscious: if I say that I am *in the winter of life*, you don't need an interpretation to understand that I am no young spring chick. But for the sake of simplicity, I will use metaphor and symbols as synonymous, because both are imaginative representations of an inner state and both give us precious information.

Although the trauma of heartbreak is archetypal, universal, and a very common drama, the image by which it is symbolized or metaphorized is unique for each person. William's metaphor of the dying turtle belongs to him alone. I don't know anyone else who has that exact same image. For William, *it is the pin on the map* that says: "You are here, this is your metaphor. You are here on the map of heartbreak: dying alone in your carapace." It locates him.

Carl Jung is probably the psychologist who best explained how attention to our emerging symbols can bring about a standpoint that transcends the previous opposition between love and freedom, puppy love and human love. Neuroscience now supports many of Jung's intuitions about the power of symbols to impact emotions even if neuroscientists have no use for Jung's poetic prose.

William is no Stendhal nor Goethe, yet his imaginary turtle was a precise symbolization of the risk of psychic death. Writing about this turtle in his notebook worked just like writing the suicide of *Young Werther*. It situated him, as if his psyche were saying, "you are psychically stuck, you are dying. Will you do something about this?" William got the message and acted on it.

The Role of Anger

William woke up one morning feeling his anger had become a sword and he was ready to break free of his emotional prison. He wrote this email to Laura:

Terminus

For ten months, I have been waiting for a clarification that you won't or can't give me. When you severed the sexual bond between us, you asked if we could remain friends. My answer is this: not now! Hope has to die off before I can see you again. I won't deny the deep affection I have for you, but for now, I want a complete severance; don't call, don't email, and don't show up. I rented out my apartment and I am leaving for a year's sabbatical.

When William wrote that final email, he had been *hooked on hope* for almost a year.[32] When his anger swelled into a tsunami, it helped him see the necessity to move away from Laura's confusing ambivalence, to avoid a possible regression to being the neglected boy of an ambivalent mother.

William is a healthy enough person, and the conclusion of his story shows how he was able to *separate*, not so much from Laura, who is basically a good-enough person, but from what, in that relationship, was unsustainable. William's awareness of his anger contained the energy to send the final email to Laura, actively breaking the bond. But anger is only a sword to cut the knot that ties you to the post.

The day after writing his last email to Laura, William went online and rented a Summerhouse in Ireland. He sent me the following email.

I read, I walk, I swim, I sleep, I heal

I read novels, I walk the cliffs with my friends, I swim with my daughters, I sleep long nights, I drink lots of tea, I cook big meals, I drink Irish beer, sing Irish songs, and I like how the world feels, with or without Laura in it. Laura's betrayal reduced me to a pathetic helpless beggar; she had that power over me because of the unconsciousness of my mother complex. Mom made me beg for her love, as if I never felt quite good enough to be worthy of it. I am free, finally!

32. The French philosopher Andre Comte-Sponville (2002) writes beautifully about the danger of living with the wrong kind of hope. He wrote a *Treatise on Despair and Bliss!* (*Traité du Désespoir et de la Béatitude!*) to argue his point.

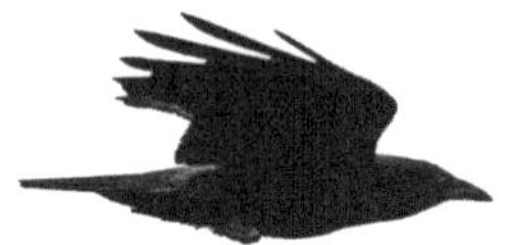

Roula-Maria Dib

Fleur de Sel

On Mediterranean salinas

Snowflakes sterilize your face with mineral mandalas
at the dinner table where Yam and Poseidon sat
sharing bread and salt.

Fleur de sel. A brackish kiss— crusts on a wound
hushing the depths into flavors of secrecy.
Mare Nostrom. Waves once a dancefloor

a spring of journeys. But now, in the rarity
of relish, water is a flammable destination.
Let the crystal dust rise, a chrysalis for the dormant.

Pantry

Sprouting beyond the mustard seed
beneath the lined eyes of fava beans
the wings of a weevil. Like mad libs
it fills in the blanks on the shelves
mixing opposite worlds. Oil
and vinegar. Sugar and chickpeas.
Clary sage and syrups.

And in between, neither East nor West
lies a land. Middle Child Syndrome.

Change sings, not in hymns but in bergamot peels
brushing a grater's lips
as flasks of pomegranate molasses hide genies
and stories in magma.
Molten gold.

Plums and almonds exist here
in double-being:
Pickled. Dried

Olive jars turned bitter
are now the salt grains
in the middle.

Simmer

Drain a hundred pouches through a colander—
thick-skinned, like villagers who soaked them:
A rattle parade of beans in the pan,
shaken awake thoughts
in a metal alembic
stainless as ink on an acetone pad.
Some cranberried, veined summer fans
of *Ayşe Khanom*.
Some original.
Pinto dressed in wild specks
obsidian eyes.
Undress a native tongue
translating
the whistles of the pressure cooker
into the soundtrack of homes.
They simmer softening into music
a gentle waltz moves the walls with transformation.

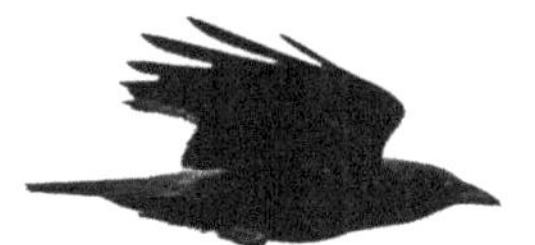

Kathy Mantas

dancing blissfully in her studio-kitchen

    the temenos—

with generosity, slices of stories,
and an abundance of nourishment
that awaken nostalgias
from childhood and ancestral m/other/land.

    the poet's invitation to *revere*—

scenes of olive trees, lavash bread baking
in ovens in the ground,
ancient sites, medieval walls, dark frescoes
the Azat valley, and village in Yeghegnadzor

    fill my imagination with possibility—

she continues her pilgrimage
scribed in cellular memory
an eggplant soul.

Mantas, K. (2022). Found poem from a book review of *The Marrow of Longing* by Celeste Nazeli Snowber. In A. Fidyk, & D. St. Georges (Eds.), Poetic Inquiry for synchrony & love: A new order of gravity [Special Issue]. *Art|Research International: A Transdisciplinary Journal, 7*(2), 564-576.

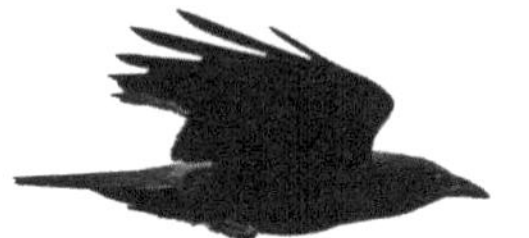

Bernie Andrews

Mum's the Word: An Immigrant's Experience[33]

Prosetry[34]

Sunday picnics
In Peterborough parks
Skipping stones
Across the Ottanabee
Walking beside Little Lake
Watching motorboats

[My first memory is of a long staircase leading up to a second-floor apartment over a store-front, orange crates for end tables, and rugs mum made from rag scraps. No matter. In Canada, unlike England, we could have our *own* roof over our heads.][35]

33. My first memory is of a long staircase leading up to a second-floor apartment over a store-front, orange crates for end tables, and rugs mum made from rag scraps. No matter. In Canada, unlike England, we could have our *own* roof over our heads.

34. Proestry is a new scholastic art-from that integrates different literary conventions, such as verse, voice (e.g., quotations), narrative, and/or commentary, to provide an audience with a multi-dimensional perspective. Prosetry provides a forum for a writer to develop ideational relationships among different forms of communication, and to convey a holistic understanding of phenomenon to a reader. This article focuses on the story of an immigrant family's experience settling in Canada after WWII. It tells of the hardships and joys experienced by the family and the mother in particular.

35. This work is an example of Prosetry which is a relatively new art form that combines various art structures to tell the story behind the story. In this selection, the verse recounts the history of the X family's immigration to Canada, and the text comments on the role that our mother played in adjusting to a new country. It was performed at Y's 90th birthday celebration by the author (verse) and his sister (text).

War-time bungalow
Hot, stuffy summers
Cold, draughty winters
Railway bridge close
Icy river flowing by
Home, sweet home

[In those days, we never really knew what caused it, but more children kept arriving. Mum ever patiently juggled the baby bottles, managed the finances, and studied music. She scrimped, saved and stretched dollars until a new, larger home was ours.]

Upscale subdivision
A twenty-five-year wage
Wooden siding
Painted fences
Marking boundaries

[I remember the old car that always needed repair and the washing machine that never worked properly. Mum was now busy teaching and performing in the community. In the absence of television, there were always lots of sing-a-longs and house parties.]

Highrise mountains
Big city lights
Ribbons of traffic
Bustle and hustle
Endless nights
Toronto the Good

[Opportunity called dad to Toronto, and mum marshalled our resources to ensure that we secured a new home. I remember the music studios in the basement, and the Pink Ladies, her female choir. They were really good looking … and they could sing!]

Real estate rising
Toronto expanding
Riding the wave northward

Scarborough sites
Unionville village
Toogood pond

[Mum always had a way with money. She knows its power is in its conservation, growth, and careful monitoring. Also, she understands real estate. Her timing was impeccable as the family moved north to Markham, and built a cottage in Muskoka.]

Golden years
Family and friends
Making music
Dancing and travel
Sing-a-long with
Bill and Joan

[During those years, I remember Paulette's many boyfriends, Robert staying out all night, Billy refusing to brush his teeth, Joan arguing with David that she was really the older twin, Susan quiet as a church mouse, and, Mum and Dad singing and dancing … always singing and dancing.]

Alone at night
Waiting forever
Staring at the light
Wishing for yesterday
Seeking resolve
To face tomorrow

[Mum lost a true friend and confidant after forty-five years of marriage when Bill Andrews passed onwards through this life and upwards to heaven. Mum rose to the occasion, and she continues to perform in churches, seniors' homes, and hospitals.]

Seven children
In-laws and out-laws
And thirteen more off-spring
Spinning a never-ending web

From but one
Starting point

[Mum seldom has a quiet word with anyone: she has an opinion on everything. But listen very carefully to what she says as her words of wisdom and insights on the human condition are invaluable, even when they are unpopular and annoyingly right!]

Coming from England
Chasing rainbows
Building a legacy
Of people
Not things
Mum's the word

Commentary

Proestry is a new scholastic art-form that integrates different literary conventions, such as verse, voice (e.g., quotations), narrative or commentary, to provide an audience with a multi-dimensional perspective. Prosetry provides a forum for a writer to develop ideational relationships among different forms of communication, and to convey a holistic understanding of phenomenon to a reader. It can be read silently by an individual, or with partners in the manner of chamber music with each person reading a different part. Alternately, it can be performed on stage for an audience solo or with partners. Further, there are different approaches to proestry. One may use commentary to inform the verse,[36] voices from the field to illuminate the narrative and verse,[37] prose to elaborate on the verse and text,[38] or narrative to convey the personal experience of the writer and the verse to capture the feelings of the experience.[39]

36. For example, Author A

37. For example, Author B and C

38. For example, Author D

39. This approach was inspired by Laurel Richardson's (1997) writing, notably *Fields of Play: Constructing An Academic Life,* Rutgers University Press. Refer to Andrews, B. W. (2000). Land of shadows. *Language and Literacy, 2*(1), http://ejournals.library.ualberta.ca/index.php/langandlit/issue/view/1351.

Proestry has it roots in the notion of alternating poetry and prose which originated in Ancient Rome and was called "manipian satire." The combining of different forms of communication within one art form re-appeared with the performance of the first opera, Jacopo Peri's Dafne, in Florence in 1597. Opera evolved into oratorio and music drama, and on the lighter side, into comic opera and musical theatre.[40] Two diverse means of communicating musical ideas—jazz improvisation and Western European musical notation—were integrated to create the swing band of the 1930s and 1940s. Combining poetry, quotations and text appeared in the work of Marshall McLuhan, although pre-dominantly as an explanatory exercise rather than an artistic one.[41] Patrick Diamond and Carol Mullen went further and experimented with a form they refer to as "palimpsest" which involves using text to represent different voices and arranging them in a variety of ways, for example by alternating columns, juxtaposition, and writing in circles and spirals.[42] Most recently, the advent of the electronic field has given rise to a range of new media, such as cell phones, television, fax, computers, digital recording and video graphics.[43] The new media has blurred the distinction among art forms and created new ways for artists to communicate. For example, we now have soap operas, television plays, epic movies, music videos and tele-journalism. Moreover, live performers, whether in the concert hall, nightclub or stadium, routinely rely on electronic media to considerable effect.[44] Proestry offers a comprehensive way to communicate feelings by combining text and verse. Further, it can also be communicated through social media, live performance, or read silently, thereby offering a range of options in delivery.

40. For a comprehensive account refer to David Ewen, *Opera: Its Story Told Through the Lives and Works of Its Foremost Composers* and Alan J. Lerner (1986), *American Musical Theatre: A Celebration.*

41. Refer to Marshall McLuhan, *From Cliché to Archetype* (Viking Press, 1970).

42. Refer to C. T. Patrick Diamond and Carol A. Mullen (Eds.) (1999), *The Post-modern educator: Arts-based Inquiries and Teacher Development*, Peter Lang.

43. Patel, M. (2012). *Wired for culture.* Norton; Robinson, K., & Aronica, L. (2016), *Creative Schools: The Grassroots Revolution that's Transforming Education.* Penguin.

44. See: Hill, B. (1998). *Going digital: A musician's guide to technology.* Schirmer; Williams, D. A. (2019). *A different paradigm in music education: Re-examining the profession.* Routledge.

Postscript

Mother
Grey-silvered hair
And well-worn hands
Eyes brimming with the memories
Of a thousand moments

You know life's cycle
Because you have lived it
Felt it, and nurtured
The seedling to its maturity
None remember the pain
The agony of many years
Of caring
None cry your glory
Bring frankincense and myrrh
Or worship at your pedestal

Yet you face the rigorous routine
Of life's living, of daily cares
With the faith, the hope
And the love
That makes a family possible

You give yourself for others
Your laurels are your progeny
Your crown their success
Your achievement their loyalty
Respect and pride
In calling you
Mother[45]

45. Mrs. Y (née Z) passed away peacefully on March 10th, 2021 in her 99th year.

Alexandra Fidyk

Small

In studying alchemy,
an ancient veiled practice,
we seek to liberate our
souls from physical attachment.

We discover dissolution—
  to break apart
  to separate by water
  to free ourselves
  from all we are not
  to become small.

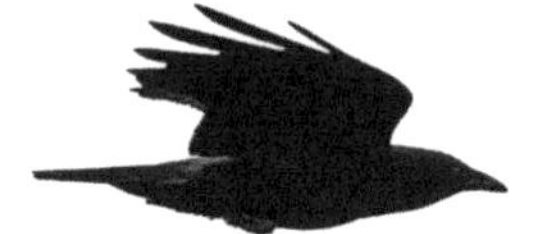

Anne McCrary Sullivan

And what is truth? Whose truth?

Tension is fertile ground for poetic expression—
a more informed witness

relationships between language and power
arise in multiple ways
building a context for genocide

many turn a blind eye
a warning for our own time—
a time when divisions are manufactured and exploited

forcing me to circle
kettling with vultures
so high I disappear.

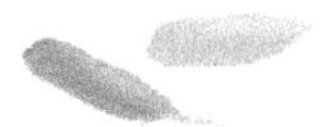

McCrary-Sullivan, A. (2022). Found poem from a book review of *Poetry, Poetic Inquiry and Rwanda: Engaging with the Lives of Others* by Laura Apol. In A. Fidyk, & D. St. Georges (Eds.), Poetic Inquiry for synchrony & love: A new order of gravity [Special Issue]. *Art|Research International: A Transdisciplinary Journal*, *7*(2), 564-576.

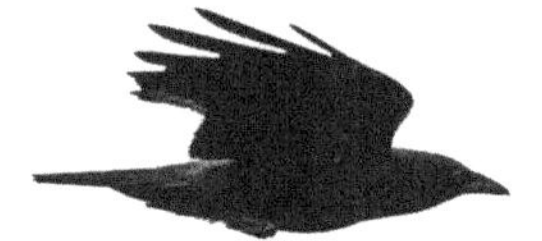

David W. Jardine

Shall We Call this "The Web of Life?"

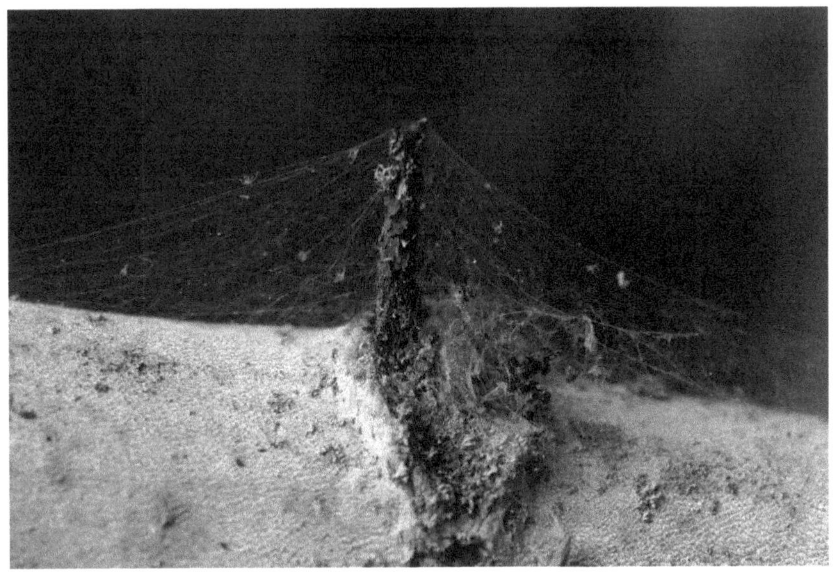

The Web of Life

Shall we call this "The Web of Life?" Of course.
Perhaps I expect too much from new
grandchildren and the exuberances of the energies that surround us.

Look closer than the eye can see. Use that other eye. Eye. Nearing. I. Coming this way. Watch out, though. As we near, vision gets better and worse. The object pixilates before our very eyes. My camera's failures feel like success, like it hides a bit if I get too intruded.

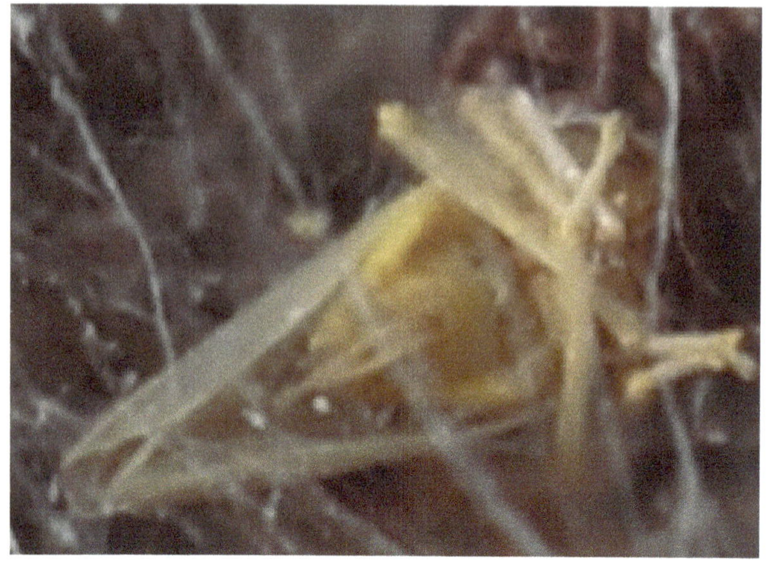

A Deep Repose. A Dead Entangle

I'm left justified, here. Life thread-wrapped. My own skin pulling in ever-softer creases. Fitting. Proper. Fair. The little heart-ache as my grandsons already outlive me. We breath and hear Preen and Groom overhead and laugh. And laugh.

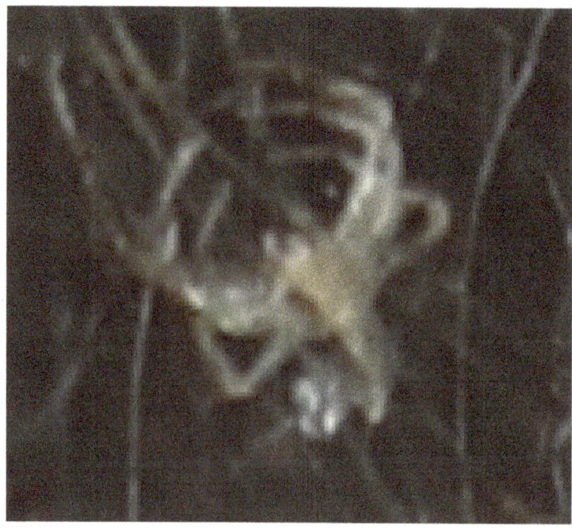

Varied. Quiet. Familiar

Weird and whitened. Very quiet. Pixel dances. What happens when pix disassemble into their elements.

Even with red headed grasshopper
arms akimbo,
eye visible,
pupil visible,
back wing still nearly greenish.
I feel somewhat spotted under that apparent lid. Looked at.

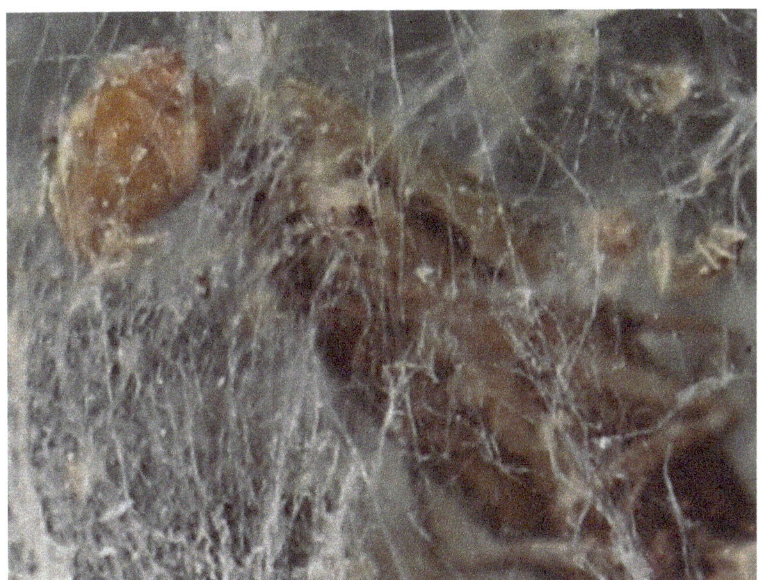

Eye Visible

And then
one
last magnification,
one last magnificence.
A pitched
silvery
battle
and the threads loosen and tighten

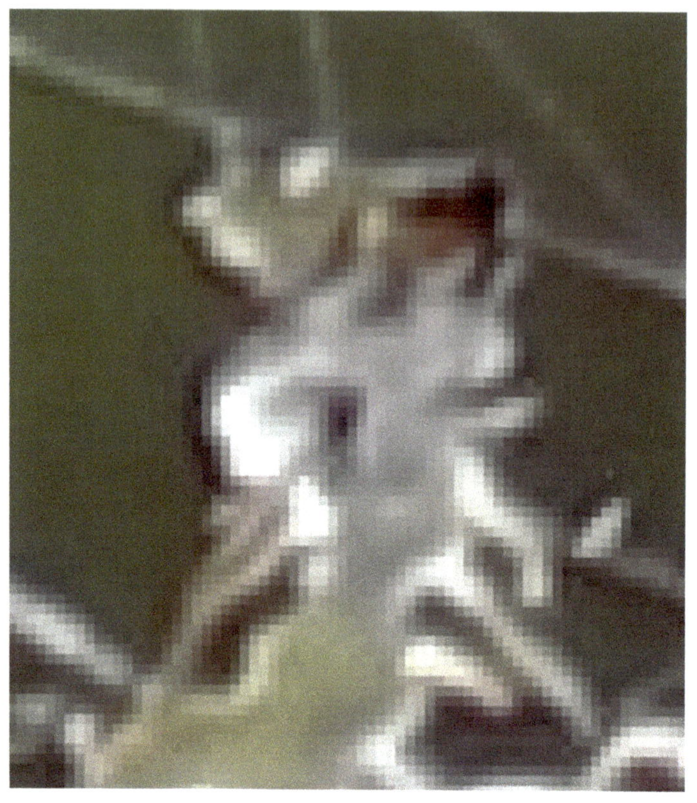

. . . the picture itself unravelling into squares
each needing to be unambiguous. This or that. See?

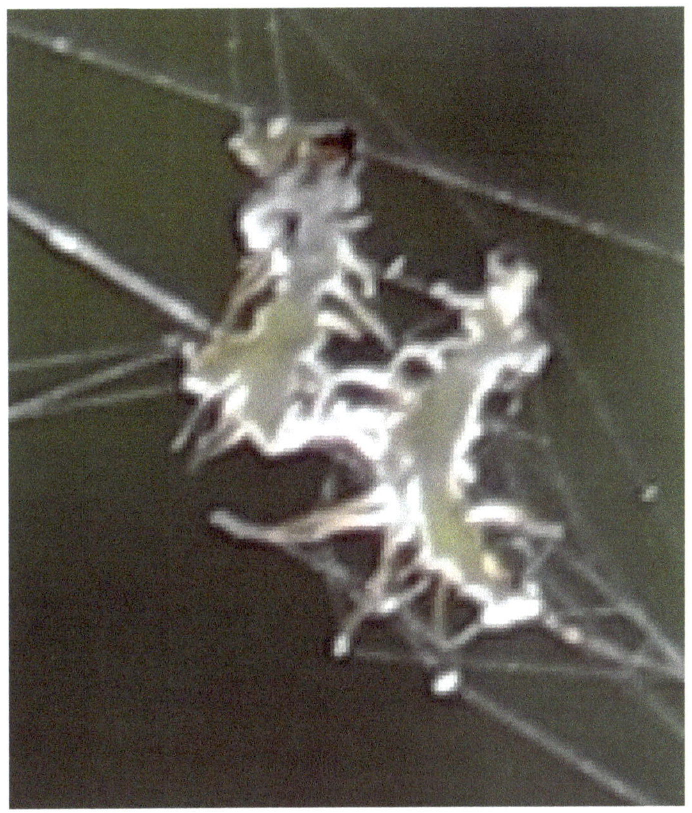

This is surely how my own attention fails as I near The Web of Life.

And this even though each picture is full of suffering, allure, imagined-dragons, and soft, sorrowful ambiguity.

The image breaks up as I near it.

I break up as I near it.

Webs on a stick on a branch. Husks betraying the struggle of living and dying.

Yes, I shall call this "The Web of Life."

Images

All photos by David W. Jardine

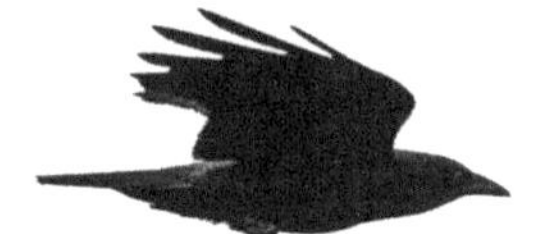

Darlene St. Georges

Stitchery

intoxicated by the aroma of newly conceived magnolia
pathways of silence fold and unfold
along an assemblage of blue hills
where tangled roots
drip, full-bodied

spilling out seeds of origins

clear chords
threading your veins

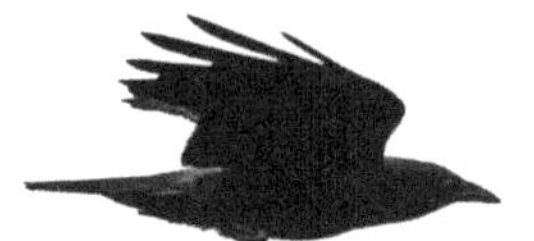

Jodi Latremouille

I once read about an ancient woman
who had no memories left to hold
but only memories—
so she danced around the old folks' home
barefoot in her too-long nightdress
cuddling and cooing to a smudge-faced plastic baby doll
wrapped in a receiving blanket
wrapped and re-wrapped many times a day
to make sure she was comfortable.
Babies like to feel secure, so we
wrap them nice and tight.
Her aging daughter once kidnapped that baby doll
and threw it in the washing machine. So callous
and practical.
Baby's matted, spiky half-melted hair
bore the hot trauma for all the world to see.
She smoothed it down with a low lullaby,
her crow hands keeping time
to the rhythm of her forgotten grief.

My daughter's neck arches back, grin wide
as she spins
around, around, and around, again.
I can see my own wiry, young-aging hands

crossing over themselves,
gripping so tightly to her smooth-padded palms,
my eyes locked in on her face as we whirl.
The blue grass swirls and blurs
but her face is frozen, shimmery-clear in the spring,
her dandelion sundress billowing out above
those familiar, knobbly, playful-bruised knees.
I am already
lost to the dream
rehearsing this day, this moment, this spin-
over, over, over, again.
Nostalgia for this moment,
for the future
that has not yet found its rhythm. Pre-emptive
grief for this
baby girl growing
out of her too-short sundress.

Credit: Reprinted from Latremouille, J. (2022). Grief-writing: Navigating ecological suffering through a relational pedagogy. In A. Fidyk, & D. St. Georges (Eds.), Poetic Inquiry for synchrony & love: A new order of gravity [Special Issue]. *Art|Research International: A Transdisciplinary Journal*, *7*(2), 439-457.

Kedrick James

'May you always be ready to say 'yes' to adventures!! . . .

Reading this conversation,
a naked investigation of lived experience through illness,
is like being pulled downstream by a river
to some great falls
marking the death of a friend and beloved mentor.

Carl's consummate compassion
an act of passing on: passing on a tradition,
an approach to knowing through writing—
living poetically and passing on
the act of dying with dignity and grace.

James, K. (2022). Found poem from A Journey to the Death: Book review of *The Spaces in Between* by Kimbe*rly Holms & Carl Leggo.* In A. Fidyk, & D. St. Georges (Eds.), Poetic Inquiry for synchrony & love: A new order of gravity [Special Issue]. *Art|Research International: A Transdisciplinary Journal, 7*(2), 554-563.

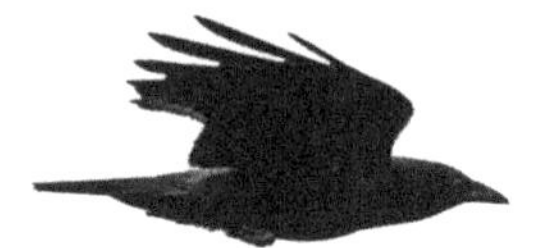

Vessela Balinska-Ourdeva

The Cave, A Place of Death & Rebirth: My Healing Journey

The Night darkens the spirit
but only to illuminate it.
—St. John of the Cross

Drip. Drip. Drip. Drip. … The IV-line measures time in a room full of people who, like me, face a difficult descent to a place where time slows down. Stops. Waits. Plumps up with patience and the knowledge of mortality. The bustle around belongs to another space, not the one I inhabit. The soul returns to knowing I do not possess but intuit, the dark feminine powers of healing and regeneration through death staring at me openly. This is the land of Ereshkigal, the ancient Sumerian goddess of the underworld (Brinton Perera, 1981). The descent to this land is usually not of one's own accord. For in our culture—sun-oriented, logos-driven, extolling the active, ego-informed ideals of unbalanced and injured yang energies—feared are patience, cessation, silence, and surrender to the Life force begetting itself in darkness.

The traditional hero story cannot help me to understand the subtle and gradual changes taking place in my ailing body, getting ready for the ultimate descent, becoming one with the "continuum in which different states are simply experienced as transformations of one energy" (Brinton Perera, 1981, p. 21). To cope is to release, to reawaken, to restore, and to revive a woman, no longer ignorant of the hurt blood my familial love oozes, as bonds with mother and grandmother create the fibers to weave a new story from the cave of my memory, from the archetypal womb of the dark moon goddess who enters the cavern in order to regenerate, to renew herself, to become fertile and give birth to herself and everything else, in a constant cycle of destruction, creation, growth, decline, death, and rebirth (George, 1992). Restorying my personal mythology starts with a journey to two actual caves that connect me directly to the ancient feminine wisdom of unity between above and below, conscious and unconscious, of processes over which I have little control "but in which I may find a grounding if [I] can reverence change itself and find [my] own way to move with it" (Brinton Perera, 1981, p. 34).

In caves, stalactites and stalagmites join to form stalagnates. From ceiling and from floor, the gradual erosion and dissolution of rocks produces new connected formations as water dissolves limestone, air releases carbon dioxide gas, redepositing calcium carbonate on the walls and insides of the cavern (National Park Service). The beginning of my latest descent dates back ten years. At that time, I was oblivious to the reality of facing a terminal illness at the age of fifty-seven. But, my body knew and revealed in dreams, spontaneous images, and poetic writing, the path I needed to follow in order to regain an "adequate sense of [my] own ground" and "connection to [my] own embodied strength and needs adequate to provide [me] with a resilient feminine, balanced yin-yang, processual ego" (Brinton Perera, 1981, p. 56). The offering here revisits the first stripping of false beliefs about my woman-being, consciously cultivated through compliance with distorted understanding of mother-love and mother-being. Seeking illumination of unconsciously held disowned values such as softness, reciprocity, warmth, gentleness, and attunement, by way of conscious retreat into the netherworld of personal trauma, I am airing wounds from the conscious rejection of my mother and grandmother, neglecting their suffering which became my suffering, and so voicing a new awareness of the necessity to reconnect with the archetypal feminine energies of the Great Goddess "as Self:" "full-bodied coherence" (p. 12) of yin-yang qualities that make up a "many-sided feminine" (p. 19).

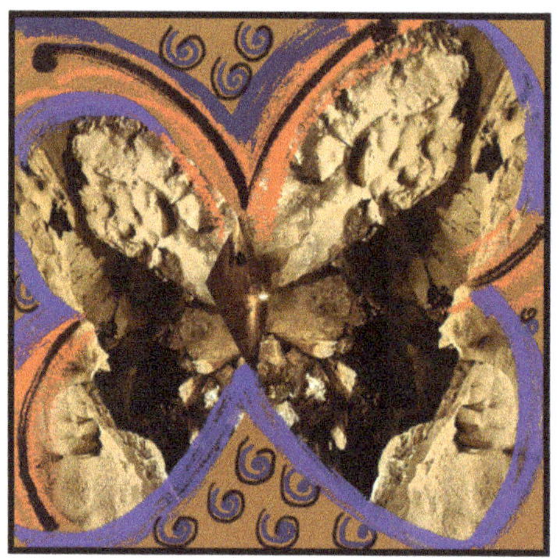

Vessela Balinska-Ourdeva, *Magura Cave Butterfly*, deconstructed photography, digital art, 2023.

An excerpt from my journal: July 16, 2009

The Magura (Rabisha) cave is magnificent. Our timing is perfect, for we arrive at 11:30 am- 12:00 pm and spend some of the hottest hours of the day in the cave. The walk through it lasts about two hours. But once in the cave, I lose any sense of ordinary time. I am fascinated with the mystery of creation, attentively observing how water patiently carves the stalactites and stalagmites, teary rocks, weeping slowly and persistently for thousands of years. The air is heavy, damp, earthy, saturated with silence and otherworld-ness.

Numerous halls and galleries make up the two-and-a-half kilometre tunnel through which we walk. The cavern is awe-inspiring. The experience of being inside is beyond any words—the shapes and colours of the rocks, the spectacular forms emerging where the water slowly has been chipping away at their surface: I don't think my writing could do justice to nature's artistry, the powerful chthonic, fecund energy emanating from the Earth's depths, taking the shapes of stones frozen in time, yet suffused with the desire for movement—constant and changeable, permanent in their gradual metamorphosis.

One particular formation leaves an irresistible impression on me, mostly because of its twisted shape—a round, textured obelisk the underground water has sculpted into a mushroom, with hair cascading silently into the darkness. Glimpses of rocks, the walls of hollow galleries barely visible, separated wombs plummeting to unknown depths. Meandering amidst them is both a frightening and an elating experience, especially when we reach the half-blocked tunnel where an avalanche of rocks has piled stone upon stone as if in a mass grave. I am relieved to be out of the mountain's belly after two hours inside the cave, the wonder of it hard to bear. Getting out of the rocky womb in the bright sunlight is striking. Literally and metaphorically, the change from darkness to light, but also the breathtaking sight outside the cave, blinds me.

The memory documents an experience I had with my parents while visiting Bulgaria in 2009, intent on reawakening supressed feelings of attachment to the land of my birth. It was a trip that also rekindled a deep connection with my parents, which over the several years between my previous and this visit seemed as if it had thinned. Particularly, the walk through the underground revived a physical bond with my mom I have not felt since childhood. I sensed her fragility and aging, but also the stamina that made her the stubborn, driven, independent woman I knew while growing up. The moments when I offered her help by gently taking her arm in mine to support her during the slippery and tricky descent into the cave's depths are palpable recollections that today make me wonder about the mystery of family ties. The closeness I felt because of the physical touch was subtle but powerful enough to recover a sense of intimacy and belonging, even though my parents and I were amidst strangers. I knew my mom by the feel of her skin, the movement of her body, the warmth her proximity brought. It felt right; it was a place where I was supposed to be.

gingerly steps
like babies just starting to walk
uncertain
my mom and I descend
into darkness more primal
than we both can understand
my body anticipating her movements
from before
the moment of birth
invisible umbilical cord—
a sacred reunion
inside an earthy underworld
mother and daughter
mother to mother
we communicate

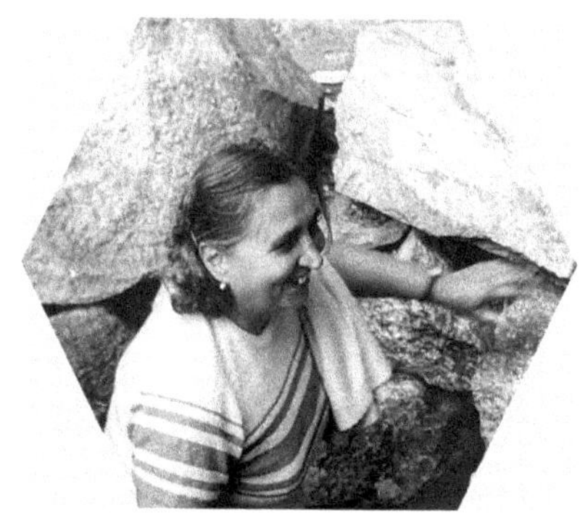

Vessela Balinska-Ourdeva, *My Grandma*, photograph, St. Ivan Rilski's Cave, Bulgaria, 2023.

A childhood memory: St. Ivan Rilski's Cave

The cave in this rumination is a sacred place. A legend holds that it was the dwelling of the first Bulgarian hermit, a saint who was famed for his purity and holy acts, his kindness and humility. The story of Ivan Rilski I learned as a child during a trip my family made to the mountain Rila where the famous cave is located.

I do not remember how old exactly I was but should not have been more than eight or nine. As we climb to its entrance, behind me I hear my grandfather's eerie storytelling voice explain that sinners were unable to crawl out of the narrow tunnel and exit the cave. Wrongdoers will get stuck and remain there for eternity, tormented by fierce devils who burn their feet and pierce their flesh with hot iron rods. Fear clutches my throat and squeezes hard as my heart begins to beat faster. I worry about myself, as I conjure up an image of the tight passage my grandfather describes; I think about my grandmother. She is a tall, heavy-set woman, with the kindest smile on earth. I worry whether she can get through. I know she is not a sinner. At that age, I do not even know what a sinner is, but in my heart of hearts, I know my grandma is not one. Yet, I am nervous as we continue to climb higher and higher into the mountain, following the well-worn path many before us have trekked.

I do not remember going into the cave and actually passing through the tunnel, but I remember my grandmother coming out of it, smiling. I remember being happy to see her stepping into the light, gentle and comforting.

I want to rush and meet her, hold her hand and walk toward the stone where we can leave our wishes for the saint to fulfill, for neither of us is a wrongdoer. Thinking about it now, I feel the connection that as a child I had with my grandma, a woman of immeasurable softness and warmth, who generously shared her wisdom and love with me. But I did not pay attention. Her voice is now silent, hidden deeply in the recesses of my memory. Still, yielding support in times of grief, torment, and profound despair.

The cave as a sacred place is a bridge between two worlds—the world of the ordinary humans and the world of the shaman who enters the underworld in order to communicate with the Great Mystery and the ancestors. In my memory, the cave is a *temenos* invoking my grandmother's presence. It is a mystical gateway I need to pass through to reunite with her spiritual energy. The cave seems to be a metaphorical space I have to fill up with words and imaginings to re-establish the connection with the woman who took care of me as a child, for my grandma practically raised me.

In both these memories, the cave is a container holding precious but unmetabolized experiences I have stored over the years. It is a sacrosanct place where I can unite with my mother and grandmother, archetypally bonded to them through my relationship with the Earth and the feminine mystique. According to Jung, in *Psychology and Alchemy*, the cave stands for "the security and impregnability of the unconsciousness" (as cited in Fraim, 2001, p. 7). Working with the image of the cave is the beginning of a journey I need to undertake, a journey that Hollis (2003) identifies as the "relocation of the ego in a larger context" (p. 14). It is, I anticipate, a form of initiation through revival of the spirit, which requires both to reconnect with my native land and to find a new appreciation for the threads that tie me to my mother and grandmother. To cite Mary Briner (2000): "the problem of self-definition … goes back to a woman's inner psychology and her relation to divergent currents and conflicts of her own feminine self" (p. 113). The relationship with my mother and grandmother I currently seek to restore suggests a relation "to what the mother has awakened in the unconscious of the daughter, which then proceeds to lead a secret life within her" (p. 113). The image of the cave is possibly asking me to recognize the yin energies in myself, which also means that I have to regress to the child I once was and resurrect her from the depth of my unconscious. The image of the cave, therefore, is an invitation.

Thinking of the heart as a cave helps me understand and acknowledge a "desire to go beneath the surface to the heart of things to discern the movement of the invisible" (Hollis, 2003, p. 18). It is a time for me to pause and witness the "Self … selving" (p. 21), which I believe will involve continuous submerging into my unconscious. In this sense, the symbol of the cave beckons me to re-examine forgotten aspects of myself, suppressed creative energies, which in the past fed into the ego, but now command a different attitude, a different imagining of how I am to be and become in the crone years of my womanhood. These are now calling, demanding attention.

"We are obliged to live the questions with whatever courage we can muster. And then, … we may live our way along into their answers" (p. 22).

the heart's chamber
is a treasure cave
guarded by a fierce dragon
one enters it
alone
knowing the magic word
that tames the beast

the chamber is alive
with air, water, stone
pulsating
reverberating,
echoing the rhythm
of the Earth
caught in a drum

heavy light **boom**-boom **boom**-boom **boom**-boom

it stores the primordial beat
of awareness—

the dark all consuming
wet, slippery, thick
blood stream
passing through it

In my experience, the cave image brings memories from the past. Entering the cave, I venture into a mysterious territory, my unconscious, which, as Stein (2005) contends, also contains "the prospects of a psychological future" (p. 10). My hope is that upon exiting the cave, I would have become a completer and more whole individual because I would have assimilated "the conscious and unconscious parts" (p. 11) of my psyche. The journey is not going to be easy, and many dangers will lurk in the dark. But the promise of wholeness achieved through the inner work of "untangling [the paradoxes of psyche], with making motives and part-selves distinct and holding them firmly in the mirror of consciousness" (p. 2) is too tempting to forsake. Heeding "the spirit of the Self" (p. 2) requires immersion in the language of *mythos*, which operates "through incarnation, by connecting bodily, erotically, relationally through story to a myth that is one of infinite in-corporations of the other through desire" (Fidyk, 2010, p. 4). Am I ready to enter the cave? My mother and grandmother beckon me to start the descent, to travel the pathway downwards to the unexplored depths of my womanhood. It is a scary undertaking but one that is necessary to see my true face, with "the shadows and the flaws, as well as the lovely parts" (Stein, 2005, p. 9). I am curious about this new woman, empowered by in-sight and freed from the clutches of my cerebral, disembodied Athena and my power-loving, tyrannical King. The call of the cave I answer, initiating a process of willful descent and wholing.

i return to the cave
in search of my full image
brokenness now
marring the body
taunting the spirit

my mother
my grandmother
calling from the depths
tell me their stories
in hushed voices

i am curious:
how did the blood run
in their bodies?
dripping
                like stalactites
                like stalagmites
                forming stalagnates
                                growing
from the floor of the Earth
to the ceiling of love

mushrooming the heart-butterfly
ready to return home
to die so the woman in me
can be reborn

Bruised Healing

cessation of desire
brings me face to face
with my bodyful desires;
my sick vessel
pleading love,
i marvel at its capacity to want
                to yearn
                to crave
despite its brokenness

has my diminished self
taken refuge in abandoning
what makes me human?

sticking to immunotherapy
treatment regiments
is it not a sign my body

is loved?
is cared for?

is able to experience herself
in longing
apart from faith,
risking her impermanence
and change?

sediments of
wishes, impulses, aspirations
limited to day-by-day,
sometimes even hourly
protraction

bite-size joys
in imitation of a healthy body:
i am careful
not to cross the boundary
of loss; bitterness &
aggression
tied into a bow
around my neck,
pendant-like

watchful
for my own projections
of suffering
and mirroring
these back to my weakened
self

ideally,
i will surrender
to her contingency
fragility
and crumbling

pensive,
my sick bodyself
assembles
her own humanity
from scraps of
primal chaos and
formless lunar forces

References

Briner, M. (2000). Mother-daughter relationship. In H. Wilmer (Ed.), *Mother Father* (pp. 107-128). Chiron Publications.

Brinton Perera, S. (1981). *Descent to the Goddess: A way of initiation for women.* Inner City Books.

Fidyk, A. (2010). Hermaphrodite as healing image: Connecting a mythic imagination to education. *Journal of Jungian Scholarly Studies, 6*(1), 1-32.

Fidyk, A. (2015). A black blessing. In D. Jardine, G. McCaffrey, & C. Gilman (Eds.), *On the pedagogy of suffering: Hermeneutic and Buddhist meditations* (pp. 101-106). Peter Lang.

Fraim, J. (2001). Cave. Symbolism of place: Natural places. http://www.symbolism.org/writing/books/sp/2/page7.html.

George, D. (1992). *Mysteries of the dark moon: The healing power of the dark goddess.* HarperCollins.

Hollis, J. (2003). *On this journey we call our life. Living the questions.* Inner City Books.

National Park Service. How stalactites and stalagmites form. *Ozark: National Scenic Riverways Missouri.* https://www.nps.gov/ozar/learn/education/speleothems.htm.

Perrucci, S. (n.d.). Dome and cave. http://www.domesintheworld.com/wp-content/uploads/2011/11/231_Italy_Perrucci_rev.pdf.

St. John of the Cross (2022) Luminour darkness. Centre for action and contemplation. Retrieved on May 2, 2024 from https://store.cac.org/products/saint-john-of-the-cross-luminous-darkness

Stein, M. (2005). Individuation: Inner work. *Journal of Jungian Theory and Practice, 7*(2), 1-13.

David W. Jardine

Preen and Groom

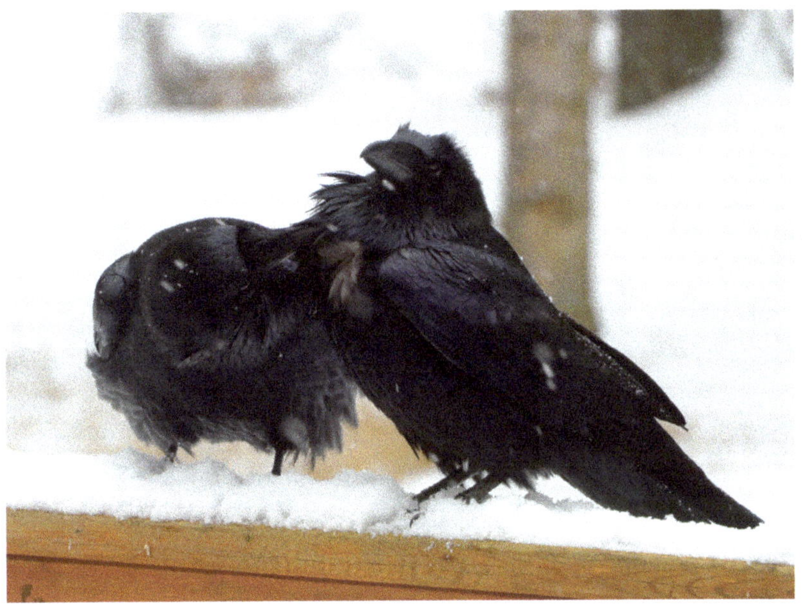

Preen and Groom.
Two names writ in fresh snow.
Now I'll take them back, these names. Ursula Le Guin's good advice.
To have lived in their curve for many years
Means I'll know if one or the other or both someday disappear.
Someday one or the other or both will disappear.

Or I will.

Not just "a pair of Ravens."
Been here years, as have I.

This originally written now 24 years ago:

> One final birding lesson for now. Catching a glimpse of a blue heron pair over past the edge of the marsh, tucked up under the willowy overhangs.
>
> Shore edge log long deep bluey sunset shadow fingers.
>
> Sudden rush of a type of recognition almost too intimate to bear, an event of birding never quite lodged in any birding guides.
>
> "It's *that* pair!"
>
> What a strange and incommensurate piece of knowledge. How profoundly, how deeply, how wonderfully *useless* it is, knowing that it is *them*, seemingly calling for names more intimate, more proper than "heron."
>
> Such knowing doesn't lead anywhere. It is, by itself, already always full, already always enough. (Jardine, 2016, p. 87)

The names more intimate are,
well, let's see.
Stop.
Notice.
Breath.
Look. Adore. Silent squawky feedings. Love.

"It's *them*." Almost too intimate to bear.

To cop what's becoming, in my bent towards age, a more and more well-worn phrase: "To be dying under their wings is a weird miracle" (Jardine, 2018, p. xiv).

Images

Photo by David W. Jardine, 2022.

References

Jardine, D. (1997). The surroundings. *Journal of Curriculum Theorizing, 13*(3), 18-21.

Jardine, D. (2016). Birding lessons and the teachings of cicadas. In D. Jardine, *In praise of radiant beings* (pp. 83-88). Information Age Press.

Jardine, D. (2018). Preface: Advice in this liquid midst. In E. Lyle (Ed.), *The negotiated self: Employing reflexive inquiry to explore teacher identity* (pp. vii-xiv). Brill Publishers.

Le Guin, U. (1987). She unnames them. In *Buffalo gals and other animal presences* (pp. 194-196). Capra Press.

Darlene St. Georges

Windswept

right there in the promised land
communicating ingenuity

Black Birds shout

punctuated with crimson sharp edges—
laying claim on your grasp of love

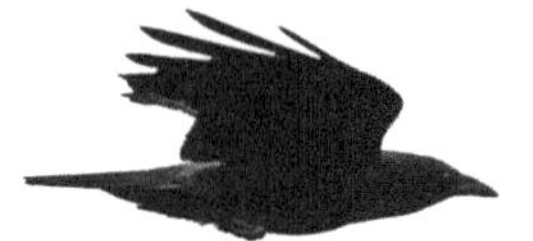

ACKNOWLEDGEMENTS

We would like to acknowledge the poetic contents of this edited collection that have been published in other collections.

Fidyk, A. (2023). "Small." In L. Crozier (Ed.), *These small hours* (p. 21). Wintergreen Studios Press.

Fidyk, A. (2023). "Our Love is a Prayer." In B. Pellman, & N. Issenman (Eds.), *How can I keep from singing?* (p. 8).

Fidyk, A. (2021). "Becoming Eve." *Journal of Jungian Scholarly Studies, Special Issue: Journey through the underworld.* https://jungianjournal.ca/index.php/jjss/issue/view/16/8

Fidyk, A. (2021). "Storyteller." *Journal of Jungian Scholarly Studies, Special Issue: Journey through the underworld.* https://jungianjournal.ca/index.php/jjss/issue/view/16/8

Fidyk, A. (2021). "The Witness." *Poiesis: A Journal of the Arts & Communication*, p. 185. http://www.egspress.com/catalogue/poiesis_vi.php

Nudelman, M. (2023). "I Shall Know Why When Time is Over," "Spirit of Survival," "Masked Regression," "Light in the Darkness of After," "Infinite Reverie," and "Skewed Perceptions." *Michael and Me.* Ekstasis Editions.

Paris, G. (2011). *Heartbreak: New approaches to healing. Recovering from lost love and mourning.* Mill City Press.

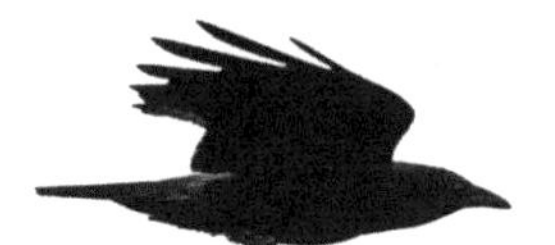

POET-AUTHORS' BIOGRAPHIES

Andrews, Bernie was Professor of Education at the University of Ottawa. He had several years of experience teaching and administering music and arts programs in school and post-secondary settings. He taught music certification and graduate courses in creativity and the arts. His research focused on educational music, interactive teaching strategies, arts partnerships, arts-based research methods, and teacher development in the arts. Bernie passed away on November 21, 2023 at the age of 73.

Andrushko, Crystal was a founding member of the Espresso Poetry Collective and is published in the anthology *Uncommon Grounds*. Her work is philosophical at heart and comes out of her regular practice of deep contemplation and unrelenting curiosity.

Apol, Laura is a widely-published poet and associate professor at Michigan State University. She is the author of several prize-winning collections of poetry, including *A Fine Yellow Dust* and most recently, *Cauterized*. Laura is a winner of the Midwest Book Award for Poetry, two-time winner of the Oklahoma Book Award, and silver-medal winner of the Independent Publishers Book Award. Her work has led her to a number of international contexts, most recently Indonesia.

Balinska-Ourdeva, Vessela, PhD, Independent Scholar, instructed in the Trauma-Sensitive Practice Graduate Certificate Program, Educational Studies, University of Alberta. Poetry, spontaneous images, and mythopoetics brought her joy, inspiring a quest for remythifying herstory. Expressive arting that bridges non-indigenous / scientific and Indigenous / animated epistemologies and memoir writing were two newly discovered passions she faithfully followed. Vessela passed away on August 23, 2024, at the age of 58 years.

Beavington, Lee is a settler-scholar of European ancestry. He is a learning strategist and interdisciplinary instructor at Kwantlen Polytechnic University, and recent recipient of KPU's Distinguished Teaching Award. He also teaches graduate students in nature-based education at Simon Fraser University. Lee serves on the Climate+ Challenge team and coordinates KPU Wild Spaces, focused on ecological place-based education. His current projects relate to decolonization, inquiry-based learning, and climate justice. More about Lee at www.wildethic.com.

Bickel, Barbara, PhD., is an artist, researcher, and educator. She is an Associate Professor of Art Education Emerita at Southern Illinois University, Core Faculty at Southwestern College, Santa Fe in the Visionary Practices and Regenerative Leadership PhD. Program, and is co-founding director of Studio M*: A Research Creation Lab Intersecting Arts, Culture, and Healing. She lives by the Salish Sea in Nanaimo, BC, Canada where she creates and teaches art as a sacred inquiry. See: http://www.barbarabickel.com and http://www.gestareartcollective

Dib, Roula-Maria is an award-winning literary scholar, poet, and editor. She is the founding director of the London Arts-Based Research Centre, founding editor of literary and arts journal, *Indelible,* and creative producer of literary event series, *Indelible Evenings*, as well as *Psychcreate*, a virtual salon on creativity and depth psychology. Her authored books include *Jungian Metaphor in Modernist Literature* (Routledge, 2020) and *Simply Being* (Chiron, 2021)

Elza, Daniela lived on three continents before immigrating to Canada in 1999. Her latest poetry collections are *the broken boat* (2020) & *slow erosions* (2020)—a chapbook written in collaboration with poet Arlene Ang. Daniela is the recipient of the 2024 Colleen Thibaudeau Award for Outstanding Contribution to Poetry. She lives on the unceded territories of the *xʷməθkʷəy̓əm* (Musqueam), Sḵwx̱wú7mesh (Squamish), and səlilwətaɬ (Tsleil-Waututh) Nations.

Davis, Megan is an Assistant Professor of Adolescence English Education at The State University of New York at New Paltz.

Fels, Lynn is a writer and Professor in Arts Education at Simon Fraser University, British Columbia. A child's tug on the sleeve while working as a freelance performing arts educator in schools in Ontario was the catalyst that initiated her doctoral journey; she theorized and articulated performative inquiry in the fledging years of arts-based research. Her research projects explore arts across the curriculum, arts for social change, performing mentorship, and performative writing.

Fidyk, Alexandra is a poet, philosopher, Jungian somatic psychotherapist, and full professor in Education at the University of Alberta. Her transdisciplinary scholarship and innovative trauma-sensitive practice graduate program integrate somatic, relational, contemplative, and arting processes, enhancing embodied presence with self and other. She remains deeply influenced by the prairie and its long sky.

halifax, nancy viva davis was born on the north shore of new brunswick on Mi'gma'gi territory \ they is a white, queer, crip poet and settler \ they is implicated in the settler colonial and nation building project of canada and works with othered others in struggle and survival within capitalist colonialism \ their most recent publication is *act normal*, McGill Queen's University Press.

Harley, James is a Master's student at the University of Alberta in English and Film Studies. They love learning through teaching and cherish experiential knowledge in knowledge production.

Holt, Regan, Dr., is a certified teacher. Dr. Holt's academic interests are transdisciplinary. Her master's degree in educational policy studies specialized in theoretical, cultural, and international studies. Her doctoral research focused on intercultural understandings of mental health for school contexts to inform curriculum and educational studies.

James, Kedrick is a poet, scholar and multi-media artist. Currently he is Director of the UBC-Okanagan School of Education. He is committed to a future in which both humans and more than humans co-exist in harmony rather than just harm. He is the developer of PhoneMe, a social media app for place-based spoken word poetry (phonemeproject.com) and Singling, a unique text sonification platform for data analysis, arts-based research, and an assistive technology for the visually impaired.

Jardine, David W. is a retired Professor Emeritus and is currently receiving a quite thorough early childhood education from his two grandsons.

John, Zena Velloo is a third generation South African Tamil from the Indian diaspora. She authored two collections of mystical poetry, "Beyond Spice" (Poets Printery, 2016) and "Sanctum" (20220—both are art and poetry anthologies featuring women visual artists. She is a ZAPP researcher, a spiritual coach, and owns an international events consultancy. She channels higher energies, writes from the ether, and transcends realms to touch eternity.

Kramer, Christi, PhD, MFA (poet and independent scholar), Under the direction of Carl Leggo at the University of British Columbia, Christi found kindred in the poetic inquiry community. Her interdisciplinary work is an exploration toward deeper understanding of poetic image as a place of meeting/crossing and the poetic imagination as a *wellspring for the building of peace.* She is a mother and teacher, loves the garden, and lives between Vancouver, BC and northern Idaho.

Latremouille, Jodi is a professor in the Faculty of Education at Vancouver Island University. She completed her doctorate in Educational Research at the University of Calgary. She also taught high school French Immersion and Social Studies. Her research interests include eco-hermeneutics, ecological, Indigenous and feminist pedagogies, social and environmental justice, life writing and poetic inquiry.

Levesque, Lauren Michelle (she/her) is an Associate Professor in the School of Leadership, Ecology, and Equity at Saint Paul University, Ottawa, Canada. Her recent works have been published in arts-focused, peer-reviewed journals such as *Music and the Arts in Action, Art/Research International,* and *Research in Drama Education.*

Levine, Stephen is the Paul Celan Chair of Philosophy and Poietics in the Arts, Health and Society Division of the European Graduate School (EGS). He is also Dean of the Doctoral Program in Expressive Arts, EGS. His primary interest lies in bringing together philosophical theory, Expressive Arts practice, and poetic inquiry within the educational framework of the EGS in order to help students find creative approaches to their professional work and to their ways of being in the world.

Lyle, Ellyn, Ph.D., has spent the last ten years in academic leadership, the past seven of which have been as Dean. During this time, she has remained active in both teaching and research. The use of critical-creative and reflexive methodologies has informed multiple publications in lived and living curriculum; intersections of self and subject and their implications for teacher and learner identity; re/humanizing education; and praxis and practitioner development. Connect with Ellyn at https://www.linkedin.com/in/ellynlyle/

MacKenzie-Dawson, Sarah is a Professor of Education at Bucknell University where she teaches courses relating to contemplative education, creativity and gender, while negotiating between her identities as a mother, scholar, teacher, poet, partner. It is the navigation within these liminal and often conflicting spaces that shapes her (re)search. Through her living, teaching and research, she embraces an epistemology that situates experience and understanding as fluid, human, imperfect, deeply complex and spiritually situated.

MacLeod, Brandon calls Thunder Bay his current home, where he writes and wanders the forests with his family and dog. He is a teacher at heart and recently completed his teaching degree in order to support and teach in the North.

Mantas, Kathy is an artist-researcher and professor of art education and graduate studies at Nipissing University, North Bay, Ontario. Her research and creative interests include: exploring nature's artistry through spontaneous and contemplative artmaking processes; creative and artful forms of inquiry; creativity in teaching-learning contexts; collaborative and artful research processes; (w)holistic and wellness education; life-long learning; women's and maternal studies.

Nudelman, Merle is a poet, educator, and lawyer. *Michael and Me* is her sixth collection of poems. Merle's first book, *Borrowed Light*, won the 2004 Canadian Jewish Book Award for Poetry. Merle's poems have been published in literary journals, anthologies, and zines in Canada and in the United States and have garnered prizes. Her academic essays appear in Canadian university publications. Merle teaches memoir and poetry writing and gives workshops on healing through words.

Oniţă, Adriana is a poet, educator, translator, editor, publisher, and researcher with a PhD in education. She is the author of two poetry chapbooks: *Misremembered Proverbs* (above/ground press, 2023) and *Conjugated Light* (Glass Buffalo, 2019). Her work has been published in CBC Books, *The Globe and Mail*, *Canthius*, *Tint Journal*, *filling Station*, and *The Humber Literary Review*. Based in Edmonton and Sicily, she is the founder of The Polyglot and the editorial director for the Griffin Poetry Prize.

Parent, Tessa is an Outreach High School teacher in the Wild Rose School Division in Alberta. She completed her MEd and Trauma Sensitive Practice graduate certificate through the University of Alberta. Serving a significant population of at-risk youth, Tessa is grateful to work in a school that allows for flexibility in providing education opportunities and socio-emotional support to meet the needs of students.

Paris, Ginette, Ph.D., is Emeritus Professor from Pacifica Graduate Institute. She the author of several books that exemplify the need for depth psychology, one of which is *Wisdom of the Psyche* (Routledge 2010, 2016). Her book about love: *Detach or Die,* 2016, conjoins Jungian and archetypal psychology with insights from neuroscience. She lectures in US, Canada and Europe. Her books have been translated in French, Spanish, Italian, German, Portuguese and Russian. Her web site is www.ginetteparis.com.

Price, Yulit is a collector of life stories and is forever humbled by the humanity she encounters both in her professional and personal life. Her work is published in *Uncommon Grounds,* an anthology by Espresso Poetry Collective. Yulit's poetry touches the therapeutic, humanistic, and socio-political threads woven into her everyday living.

Rallis, Nicole is a PhD candidate in curriculum studies and art education at University of British Columbia. Her research interests include a/r/tography, poetic inquiry, embodied learning and land-based pedagogies. Nicole's dissertation investigates the ways that in-service art teachers in the Cowichan Valley are artfully engaging with the lands they work, live, and create with to think through important social, political, ecological, and cultural issues. She is a co-editor of the book *Walking in Art Education: Ecopedagogical & A/r/tographical Encounter.*

Reis, Patricia is the author of the newly released work of historic fiction, *Unsettled* (Sybilline Press, year 2023). Her memoir, *Motherlines: Love, Longing, and Liberation* (She Writes Press, 2016) won a gold medal for memoir from Independent Press Publishers. Along with numerous essays and reviews, she has published several nonfiction books. Reis holds a BA in English Literature from the University of Wisconsin, an MFA from UCLA and a degree in Depth Psychology from Pacifica Graduate Institute in Santa Barbara.

Seidel, Jackie is an Associate Professor of Curriculum and Learning at the University of Calgary. She is passionate about exploring the existential and pedagogical meanings of ecological and social justice issues with teachers, including the climate and nature crisis. As a certified Mindfulness Based Stress Reduction

(MBSR) instructor, Jackie seeks to integrate ecological, relational, and pedagogical wellbeing throughout her work. She is learning Arabic, and enjoys writing poetry, knitting socks, bikes, and bees.

Snowber, Celeste Nazeli, PhD is a dancer, poet, writer, and award-winning educator who is a Professor in the Faculty of Education at Simon Fraser University. She has published and performed widely, and her books include Embodied inquiry, three collections of poetry and her most recent book is Dance, place, and poetics: Site-specific performance as a portal to knowing. Celeste creates site-specific performance and can be found dancing between land and sea and at www.celestesnowber.com.

Stewart, Sheila grew up on the lands of Haudenosaunee, Anishnawbe, Ojibway /Chippewa, and Neutral Peoples in Southwestern Ontario as a second generation Irish-Canadian. Her poetry collections are *A Hat to Stop a Train*, *The Shape of a Throat*, and most recently *If I Write About My Father*. She co-edited *The Art of Poetic Inquiry* (Backalong Books, 2012).

St. Georges, Darlene is a creation-centred artist | scholar. She is associate professor of art education at the University of Lethbridge, Alberta, Canada. Her theoretical and practice-based scholarship is rooted in emergent and generative knowledge and knowing that honours the inward and creative ways of being—living literacies expressed through aesthetic translation of voice, breath, body, and spirit. Her poetry has been published nationally and internationally. Darlene is co-editor of *Artizein: Arts and Teaching Journal*. See: www.darlenestgeorges.com Contact: darlene.stgeorges@uleth.ca

Vinz, Ruth is Morse Endowed Professor of English Education at Teachers College, Columbia University. In this fifty-eighth year of teaching, Vinz believes encounters with poetry open spaces to nurturer empathy, imagination, and curiosity. Poetry is a gift—haunting us, chiding us to keep feeling and imagining—vibrant within us.

Walsh, Susan, as a woman of European settler heritage, lives with gratitude on Métis Region 4 land and Treaty 6 territory—traditional home of many Indigenous people, including the Nehiyaw (Cree), Denesuliné (Dene), and Nakota Sioux (Stoney). Susan is a mother, grandmother, poet-artist, teacher, and Professor Emerita, Mount Saint Vincent University. Currently, she devotes time to writing, meditation, photography, and making friends with the land and wider writing community. Please see selected publications at https://www.msvu.ca/academics/faculty-of-education/faculty-profiles/dr-susan-walsh/

Weiss, Karen has taught in the Northern Peace Country for over forty years. She calls Silver Valley her home, where she enjoys the company of her grandchildren and the animals that make their way into her home and heart.

Weiss, Melaina is a PhD student at the University of Alberta in the department of Secondary Education. Her research is in rural education and she embraces creative, artistic, poetic, and improvisation in research technique.

Wentworth, Annette, a poet, author, and essayist, is currently completing her PhD on rural women's lived experience and the (dis)remembrance of AIDS in South Africa. She is the co-chair of the Memory Studies Association Africa regional group and affiliated with the Centre for the Study of the Afterlife of Violence and the Reparative Quest (AVReQ), Stellenbosch University. Originally from Canada, Annette has spent the majority of her time in Southern Africa for over 20 years.

www.ingramcontent.com/pod-product-compliance
Lightning Source LLC
LaVergne TN
LVHW051938100826
845154LV00002B/18
9781966214304